D0188360

HOPE

90 DEVOTIONS FROM
OUR DAILY BREAD

COMPILED BY DAVE BRANON

Our Daily Bread
Publishing™

CONTENTS

FOREWORD

American poet Emily Dickinson painted a beautiful word picture of hope when she wrote,

> *Hope is the thing with feathers*
> *That perches in the soul—*
> *And sings the tunes without the words*
> *And never stops at all.*

Miss Dickinson correctly captured the essence of true hope when she said it "never stops at all." Hope is the ongoing realization in our hearts that things can get better, that Someone other than us has things under control, and that whatever bad thing we are enduring—something better lies ahead.

Here's an example of how hope can lift up the heart of one who is facing seemingly insurmountable hopelessness. In Psalm 3, King David has just discovered that his son Absalom—after a four-year-long propaganda campaign to undermine David (2 Samuel 15)—has mounted an army to take over the throne. "How many are my foes!" David says (Psalm 3:1) as he realizes the seriousness of the threat. And he has heard that the people of Israel have concluded, "God will not deliver him" (v. 2).

Yet despite facing an attempted coup by his own son, David praises God, whom the king calls "a shield around me" (v. 3). He also realizes that when he calls out for help, God "answers me from his holy mountain" (v. 4). And he concludes that "the LORD sustains me" (v. 5) and "from the LORD comes deliverance" (v. 8).

David understood that with God hope "never stops at all." We can always have confidence that our heavenly Father, who cares for even tiny birds, cares deeply for us.

Within the pages of this book of articles by the *Our Daily Bread* writers is a collection of wisdom from God's Word about the concept of hope. It is our desire that if you are facing situations in which you feel discouraged or disenchanted or disadvantaged because of your life circumstances, you can turn to these pages and be reminded that help and encouragement are on the way. As you read these articles and are reminded of the never-ending care of the heavenly Father in your life, "may the God of hope fill you with all joy and peace as you trust in him, so that you may overflow with hope by the power of the Holy Spirit" (Romans 15:13).

—*Dave Branon*
Our Daily Bread writer

HOPEFUL REALISTS

Read: Micah 7:1-13

I will bear the LORD's wrath . . . He will bring me out into the light;
I will see his righteousness. —MICAH 7:9

A humorist wrote, "When I was feeling down, someone told me, 'Cheer up, things could get worse.' So I cheered up—and they did!"

Wishing someone a shallow "cheer up" seldom helps that person's distress. What people long for is reassuring news that life will soon change for the better. During my years as a pastor, though, I often had to tell very ill people that unless the Lord intervened they would soon die. That's hardly "cheer up" news.

In Micah's day, many people in Israel no doubt wanted to hear some good news. The ruthlessness and dishonesty of fellow-citizens, rulers, and even judges were frightening (Micah 7:2-3). The nation was so fractured that people could not even trust their closest friends or relatives (vv. 5-6). The decent citizens hoped the prophet would tell them that a revival was coming to bring positive changes in their land. Instead, he had to tell them that God's judgment was at hand: The Assyrians would soon invade.

The outlook was gloomy. But it was not hopeless. Micah saw beyond the judgment to a time when the nation would worship God and be blessed. He was mixing realism with hope. We too can be hopeful realists. With the eye of faith we can see through the hard times and see the eternal glory God has in store for us.

—*Herb Vander Lugt*

Sorrow looks back, worry looks around, but faith looks up.

LITTLE LIES AND KITTENS

Read: Romans 5:12-21

Just as sin ruled over all people and brought them to death, now God's wonderful grace rules instead. —ROMANS 5:21 NLT

Mom noticed four-year-old Elias as he scurried away from the newborn kittens. She had told him not to touch them. "Did you touch the kitties, Elias?" she asked. "No!" he said earnestly. So Mom had another question: "Were they soft?"

"Yes," he volunteered, "and the black one mewed."

With a toddler, we smile at such duplicity. But Elias's disobedience underscores our human condition. No one has to teach a four-year-old to lie. "For I was born a sinner," wrote David in his classic confession, "yes, from the moment my mother conceived me" (Psalm 51:5 NLT). The apostle Paul said: "When Adam sinned, sin entered the world. Adam's sin brought death, so death spread to everyone, for everyone sinned" (Romans 5:12 NLT). That depressing news applies equally to kings, four-year-olds, and you and me.

But there's plenty of hope! "God's law was given so that all people could see how sinful they were," wrote Paul. "But as people sinned more and more, God's wonderful grace became more abundant" (Romans 5:20 NLT).

God is not waiting for us to blow it so He can pounce on us. He is in the business of grace, forgiveness, and restoration. We need only recognize that our sin is neither cute nor excusable and come to Him in faith and repentance.

—*Tim Gustafson*

There is now no condemnation for those who are in Christ Jesus.
—Romans 8:1

WHEN MORNING COMES

Read: Hebrews 11:1-8

Now faith is confidence in what we hope for and assurance about what we do not see. —HEBREWS 11:1

It was very late when my husband and I stopped for the night at a country inn outside of Munich, Germany. We were delighted to see that our cozy room had a balcony, although an oppressive fog made it impossible to see into the darkness. But when the sun rose a few hours later, the haze began to fade. Then we could see what had been grimly shrouded the night before—a completely idyllic scene—peaceful and lush green meadows, sheep grazing with tiny tinkling bells about their necks, and big white clouds in the sky that looked exactly like more sheep—*huge*, fluffy sheep!

Sometimes life can get clouded over by a heavy fog of despair. Our situation may look so dark that we begin to lose hope. But just as the sun burns away a fog, our faith in God can burn away the haze of doubt. Hebrews 11 defines faith as "confidence in what we hope for and assurance about what we do not see" (v. 1). The passage goes on to remind us of the faith of Noah, who was "warned about things not yet seen," yet obeyed God (v. 7). And it reminds us of Abraham, who went where God directed even though he didn't know where that would be (v. 8).

Though we have not seen God and cannot always feel His presence, He is always present and will help us through our darkest nights.

—*Cindy Hess Kasper*

———

Faith is the radar that sees through the fog. —Corrie ten Boom

THE LAND OF WHAT IS

Read: Psalm 46:1-7

Brothers and sisters, we do not want you to be uninformed about those who sleep in death, so that you do not grieve like the rest of mankind, who have no hope. —1 THESSALONIANS 4:13

Even all these years after losing our seventeen-year-old daughter Melissa in a car accident in 2002, I sometimes find myself entering the world of "What If." It's easy, in grief, to reimagine the events of that tragic June evening and think of factors that—if rearranged—would have had Mell arriving safely home.

In reality, though, the land of "What If" is not a good place to be for any of us. It is a place of regret, second-guessing, and hopelessness. While the grief is real and the sadness endures, life is better and God is honored if we dwell in the world of "What Is."

In that world, we can find hope, encouragement, and comfort. We have the sure hope (1 Thessalonians 4:13)—the assurance—that because Melissa loved Jesus she is in a place that is "better by far" (Philippians 1:23). We have the helpful presence of the God of all comfort (2 Corinthians 1:3). We have God's "ever-present help in trouble" (Psalm 46:1). And we often have the encouragement of fellow believers.

We all wish to avoid the tragedies of life. But when we do face hard times, our greatest help comes from trusting God, our sure hope in the land of What Is.

—Dave Branon

Our greatest hope
comes from trusting God.

)(

HIS PLAN OR OURS?

Read: 1 Chronicles 17:1-20

Then King David went in and sat before the LORD, and he said: "Who am I, LORD God, and what is my family, that you have brought me this far?"
—1 CHRONICLES 17:16

When my husband was eighteen years old, he started a car-cleaning business. He rented a garage, hired helpers, and created advertising brochures. The business prospered. His intention was to sell it and use the proceeds to pay for college, so he was thrilled when a buyer expressed interest. After some negotiations, it seemed that the transaction would happen. But at the last minute, the deal collapsed. It wouldn't be until several months later that his plan to sell the business would succeed.

It's normal to be disappointed when God's timing and design for our lives do not match our expectations. When David wanted to build the Lord's temple, he had the right motives, the leadership ability, and the resources. Yet God said he could not undertake the project because he had killed too many people in battle (1 Chronicles 22:8).

David could have shaken his fist at the sky in anger. He could have pouted or plowed ahead with his own plans. But he humbly said, "Who am I, LORD God . . . that you have brought me this far?" (17:16). David went on to praise God and affirm his devotion to Him. He valued his relationship with God more than his ambition.

What is more important—achieving our hopes and dreams, or our love for God?

—*Jennifer Benson Schuldt*

True satisfaction is found in yielding ourselves to the will of God.

WHEN THE WOODS WAKE UP

Read: John 11:14-27

Jesus said . . . , "I am the resurrection and the life. Whoever believes in me, though he die, yet shall he live." —JOHN 11:25 ESV

Through cold, snowy winters, the hope of spring sustains those of us who live in Michigan. May is the month when that hope is rewarded. The transformation is remarkable. Limbs that look lifeless on May 1 turn into branches that wave green leafy greetings by month's end. Although the change each day is imperceptible, by the end of the month the woods in my yard have changed from gray to green.

God has built into creation a cycle of rest and renewal. What looks like death to us is rest to God. And just as rest is preparation for renewal, death is preparation for resurrection.

I love watching the woods awaken every spring, for it reminds me that death is a temporary condition and that its purpose is to prepare for new life, a new beginning, for something even better. "Unless a kernel of wheat falls to the ground and dies, it remains only a single seed. But if it dies, it produces many seeds" (John 12:24).

While pollen is a springtime nuisance when it coats my furniture and makes people sneeze, it reminds me that God is in the business of keeping things alive. And after the pain of death, He promises a glorious resurrection for those who believe in His Son.

—Julie Ackerman Link

———

Every new leaf of springtime is a reminder of our promised resurrection.

START FRESH

Read: Psalm 86:5-15

His compassions never fail. They are new every morning;
great is your faithfulness. —LAMENTATIONS 3:22–23

When I was growing up, one of my favorite books was *Anne of Green Gables* by Lucy Maud Montgomery. In one amusing passage, young Anne, by mistake, adds a skin medication instead of vanilla to the cake she is making. Afterward, she exclaims hopefully to her stern-faced guardian, Marilla, "Isn't it nice to think that tomorrow is a new day with no mistakes in it yet?"

I like that thought: tomorrow is a new day—a new day when we can start afresh. We all make mistakes. But when it comes to sin, God's forgiveness is what enables us to start each morning with a clean slate. When we repent, He chooses to remember our sins no more (Jeremiah 31:34; Hebrews 8:12).

Some of us have made wrong choices in our lives, but our past words and deeds need not define our future in God's eyes. There is always a fresh start. When we ask for His forgiveness, we take a first step toward restoring our relationship with Him and with others. "If we confess our sins, he is faithful and just and will forgive us our sins and purify us from all unrighteousness" (1 John 1:9).

God's compassion and faithfulness are new every morning (Lamentations 3:23), so we can start fresh each day.

—*Cindy Hess Kasper*

Each new day gives us new reasons to praise the Lord.

THIS COULD BE THE YEAR

Read: 1 Thessalonians 4:13-18

We who are still alive and are left will . . . meet the Lord in the air.
And so we will be with the Lord forever.
—1 THESSALONIANS 4:17

My dad was a pastor, and on the first Sunday of each new year he preached about the return of Christ, often quoting from 1 Thessalonians 4. His point was always the same: "This could be the year Jesus will return. Are you ready to meet Him?" I'll never forget hearing that sermon at age six, thinking, *If that's true, I'm not sure I will be among those He's coming for.* I felt certain that my parents would be going to heaven, and I wanted to go too. So, when my dad came home after church, I asked how I could be sure. He opened the Bible, read some verses to me, and talked to me about my need for a Savior. It didn't take much to convince me of my sins. That day, my dad led me to Christ. I will be forever grateful to him for planting these truths in my heart.

In an increasingly chaotic world, what a hopeful thought that this could be the year Jesus returns! More comforting still is the anticipation that all who trust Him for salvation will be gathered together, relieved from this world's suffering, sorrow, and fear. Best of all, we'll be with the Lord forever!

—*Joe Stowell*

——

Perhaps today! —Dr. M. R. DeHaan

HOPE IS FOR . . .

Read: Hebrews 10:19-25

Let us hold unswervingly to the hope we profess,
for he who promised is faithful. —HEBREWS 10:23

Although I try not to be shocked by the things I see these days, I was caught off-balance by the message on the woman's T-shirt as she walked past me in the mall. The bold letters declared: "Hope Is For Suckers." Certainly, being naïve or gullible can be foolish and dangerous. Disappointment and heartache can be the tragic offspring of unfounded optimism. But not allowing oneself to have hope is a sad and cynical way to view life.

Biblical hope is unique; it's a confident trust in God and what He is doing in the world and in our lives. That's something everyone needs! The writer to the Hebrews clearly stated the importance of hope when he wrote, "Let us hold unswervingly to the hope we profess, for he who promised is faithful" (Hebrews 10:23).

Having biblical hope is not foolish, because it has a strong foundation. We hold fast to the hope we have received in Christ because our God is faithful. He can be trusted with anything and everything we will ever face—both for today and forever. Our hope is grounded in the trustworthy character of the God who loves us with an everlasting love. So, the T-shirt had it wrong. Hope is not for suckers; it's for you and for me!

—*Bill Crowder*

Hope that has its foundation in God will not crumble under the pressures of life.

X

CHRIST THE REDEEMER

Read: Job 19:23-29

I know that my redeemer lives. —JOB 19:25

The famous statue *Christ the Redeemer* overlooks the city of Rio de Janeiro. The statue is a model of Christ with His arms extended so that His body forms the shape of a cross. Brazilian architect Heitor da Silva Costa designed the figure. He imagined that the city's residents would see it as the first image to emerge from the darkness at dawn. At dusk, he hoped the city dwellers would view the setting sun as a halo behind the statue's head.

There is value in keeping our eyes on our Redeemer each day—during the good times and the difficult times. As he suffered, Job said, "I know that my redeemer lives, and that in the end he will stand on the earth" (Job 19:25).

The cry of Job's heart points us to Jesus—our living Savior who will visit the earth again one day (1 Thessalonians 4:16–18). Keeping our eyes on Jesus means remembering that we have been rescued from our sin. Jesus "gave himself for us to redeem us from all wickedness and to purify for himself a people that are his very own" (Titus 2:14).

Anyone who has accepted Jesus as Savior has a reason to be glad today. No matter what we endure on earth, we can have hope today and look forward to enjoying eternity with Him.

—*Jennifer Benson Schuldt*

Through His cross and resurrection, Jesus rescues and redeems.

HABITS OF A HEALTHY MIND

Read: Psalm 37:1-8

Trust in the Lord and do good. —PSALM 37:3

There is much said today about improving our health by developing habits of optimism, whether facing a difficult medical diagnosis or a pile of dirty laundry. Dr. Barbara Fredrickson, a psychology professor at the University of North Carolina, says we should try activities that build joy, gratitude, love, and other positive feelings. We know, however, that more is required than a general wish for good feelings. We need a strong conviction that there is a source of joy, peace, and love upon which we can depend.

Psalm 37:1–8 gives positive actions we can take as an antidote to pessimism and discouragement. Consider these mood boosters: Trust in the Lord, do good, dwell in the land, feed on His faithfulness (v. 3); delight in the Lord (v. 4); commit your way to the Lord, trust in Him (v. 5); rest in the Lord, wait patiently for Him, do not fret (v. 7); cease from anger, forsake wrath (v. 8).

Because they are connected to the phrase "in the Lord," those directives are more than wishful thinking or unrealistic suggestions. It's because of Jesus, and in His strength, that they become possible.

Our one true source for optimism is the redemption that is in Jesus. He is our reason for hope!

—*David McCasland*

When there's bad news, our hope is the good news of Jesus.

IS THERE HOPE?

Read: Matthew 28:1-10

"He is not here; he has risen, just as he said."
—MATTHEW 28:6

I sat quietly at the graveside of my father, waiting for the private family burial of my mother to begin. The funeral director carried the urn that held her ashes. My heart felt numb and my head was in a fog. How can I handle losing them both within just three months? In my grief I felt loss and loneliness, and I felt a little hopeless facing a future without them.

Then the pastor read about another graveside. On the first day of the week, early in the morning, women went to Jesus's tomb, carrying spices for His body (Matthew 28:1; Luke 24:1). There they were startled to find an open and empty tomb— and an angel. "Do not be afraid," he said to them (Matthew 28:5). They didn't need to be afraid of the empty tomb or of the angel, because he had good news for them.

Hope stirred when I heard the next words: "He is not here; he has risen, just as he said" (v. 6). Because Jesus had come back to life, death had been conquered! Jesus reminded His followers just a few days before His death: "Because I live, you also will live" (John 14:19).

Even though we grieve at the loss of our loved ones, we find hope through the resurrection of Jesus and His promise that there is life after death.

—*Anne Cetas*

Because He lives, we live.

NEW BEGINNINGS

Read: Isaiah 43:14-21

See, I am doing a new thing! Now it springs up; do you not perceive it?
—ISAIAH 43:19

New beginnings are possible. Just ask Brayan, a young man who joined a gang in elementary school. Brayan ran away when he was twelve years old, and for three years he was lost in gang and drug life. Although he left the gang and returned home, it was difficult for him, as he had been expelled from school for selling drugs. When he enrolled in a new high school, however, a teacher inspired and encouraged him to write about his experiences rather than repeat them. He embraced the challenge and is now experiencing a fresh start.

God, through the prophet Isaiah, encouraged Jewish exiles to think about a new beginning as well. God said, "Forget the former things; do not dwell on the past" (Isaiah 43:18). He told them to stop dwelling on their punishment and even on His display of power through the original exodus from Egypt. He wanted their attention to be focused on God, who would give them a new beginning by bringing them home from Babylon through a new exodus (v. 19).

With God, new beginnings are possible in our hearts. He can help us to let go of the past and start clinging to Him. A relationship with Him provides a new hope for all who will trust Him.

—*Marvin Williams*

———

Let God have your life; He can do more with it than you can.

SINGING WITH VIOLET

Read: Philippians 1:21–26

I desire to depart and be with Christ, which is better by far;
but it is more necessary for you that I remain in the body.
—PHILIPPIANS 1:23–24

An elderly woman named Violet sat on her bed in a Jamaican infirmary and smiled as some teenagers stopped to visit with her. The hot, sticky, midday air came into her little group home unabated, but she didn't complain. Instead, she began wracking her mind for a song to sing. Then a huge smile appeared and she sang, "I am running, skipping, jumping, praising the Lord!" As she sang, she swung her arms back and forth as if she were running. Tears came to those around her, for Violet has no legs. She was singing because, she said, "Jesus loves me—and in heaven I will have legs to run with."

Violet's joy and hopeful anticipation of heaven give new vibrancy to Paul's words in Philippians 1 when he referred to life-and-death issues. "If I am to go on living in the body, this will mean fruitful labor for me," he said. "I am torn between the two: I desire to depart and be with Christ, which is better by far" (vv. 22–23).

Each of us faces tough times that may cause us to long for the promise of heavenly relief. But as Violet showed us joy despite her current circumstances, we too can keep "running, skipping, praising the Lord"—both for the abundant life He gives us here and for the ultimate joy that awaits us.

—*Dave Branon*

When God gives us a new beginning, we find a joy that's never ending.

HOPE IN SUFFERING

Read: 1 Peter 1:3-9

In this [living hope] you greatly rejoice, though now for a little while
you may have had to suffer grief in all kinds of trials.
—1 PETER 1:6

When I opened my Bible to read Jeremiah 1 through 4, the subhead ascribed to the book startled me: "Hope in Time of Weeping." I almost cried. The timing was perfect, as I was walking through a season of weeping over the death of my mom.

I felt much the same way after hearing my pastor's sermon the day before. The title was "Joy in Suffering," taken from 1 Peter 1:3–9. He gave us an illustration from his own life: the one-year anniversary of his father's death. The sermon was meaningful for many, but for me it was a gift from God. These and other events were indications backed up by His Word that God would not leave me alone in my grief.

Even though the way of sorrow is hard, God sends reminders of His enduring presence. To the Israelites expelled from the Promised Land due to disobedience, God made His presence known by sending prophets like Jeremiah to offer them hope—hope for reconciliation through repentance. And to those He leads through times of testing, He shows His presence through a community of believers who "love one another deeply, from the heart" (1 Peter 1:22). These indications of God's presence during trials on earth affirm God's promise of the living hope awaiting us at the resurrection.

—*Julie Ackerman Link*

We need never be ashamed of our tears.

QUIET CONVERSATIONS

Read: Psalm 116:5-9

Praise the LORD, my soul, and forget not all his benefits.
—PSALM 103:2

Do you ever talk to yourself? Sometimes when I'm working on a project—usually under the hood of a car—I find it helpful to think aloud, working through my options on the best way to make the repair. If someone catches me in my "conversation" it can be a little embarrassing—even though talking to ourselves is something most of us do every day.

The psalmists often talked to themselves in the Psalms. The author of Psalm 116 is no exception. In verse 7 he writes, "Return to your rest, my soul, for the LORD has been good to you." Reminding himself of God's kindness and faithfulness in the past is a practical comfort and help to him in the present. We see "conversations" like this frequently in the Psalms. In Psalm 103:1 David tells himself, "Praise the LORD, my soul; all my inmost being, praise his holy name." And in Psalm 62:5 he affirms, "Yes, my soul, find rest in God; my hope comes from him."

It's good to remind ourselves of God's faithfulness and the hope we have in Him. We can follow the example of the psalmists and spend some time naming the many ways God has been good to us. As we do, we'll be encouraged. The same God who has been faithful in the past will continue His love for us in the future.

—James Banks

Reminding ourselves about God's goodness can keep us filled with His peace.

THE ANCHOR OF OUR HOPE

Read: Hebrews 6:13-20

We have this hope as an anchor for the soul, firm and secure.
—HEBREWS 6:19

Frank, Ted, and I were fishing for bluegill on Rice Lake in Ontario, Canada. We were on a pontoon boat, and the fish were really biting. Busy baiting and hooking, we slowly became aware that the action had slacked off. Then we realized why: The boat was no longer sitting where we had put it. A strong wind had come up and pushed it across the water. The anchor could not hold us and was sliding across the lake bottom. We hauled it up, returned to our hot spot, and re-anchored. We were moved away again. After a third try, we went back to shore. We could not get our anchor to grab and stick.

When it comes to our salvation, our hope is anchored in the promise of God and the work of Jesus Christ. The winds and waves of doubt, discouragement, and spiritual attack by the evil one can cause us to think that we are adrift and that salvation from God is not secure. Not so! God has given His promise that our salvation is sure, and He cannot lie (Hebrews 6:18–19). Our hope is securely fastened in Jesus Christ, who redeemed us once and for all when He died, rose again, and ascended to heaven.

Our anchor is the Rock unmovable—Jesus Christ. His limitless love holds us sure and steadfast.

—*David Egner*

———

Our anchor is the Rock, Jesus Christ.

THE CHALLENGE
OF CONFINEMENT

Read: Jeremiah 29:4-14

Grow in the grace and knowledge of our Lord and Savior Jesus Christ.
—2 PETER 3:18

At the age of 86, Ken Deal concluded more than three decades of volunteer jail and prison ministry with a final Sunday sermon. His message to the inmates was about serving the Lord while incarcerated. Many of the examples he used came from prisoners, some serving life sentences. In a place everyone wants to leave, he encouraged them to grow and to share the good news of Jesus Christ with others.

After the people of Judah were taken captive by King Nebuchadnezzar and deported to Babylon because of their disobedience to God, the prophet Jeremiah sent them this message from the Lord: "Build houses and settle down; plant gardens and eat what they produce. Marry and have sons and daughters; find wives for your sons and give your daughters in marriage . . . . Increase in number there; do not decrease" (Jeremiah 29:5–6).

We may face some limiting circumstance today. Whether it is the result of our failure, or through no fault of our own, we can "go" through it or seek God's strength to "grow" through it. The challenge of every confinement is to increase rather than decrease—to grow and not diminish. The Lord's goal is to give us "hope and a future" (v. 11).

—*David McCasland*

A limited situation may afford the soul a chance to grow.

THE BEST LIFE

Read: John 1:35-42

The first thing Andrew did was to find his brother Simon and tell him, "We have found the Messiah." —JOHN 1:41

A few months ago, I had to travel to Florida and back on business. On my flight home, I was pleasantly surprised to find that I had a seat with lots of legroom. It felt so good not to be scrunched into a small area. Plus, I had an empty seat beside me! The makings of a good nap.

Then I remembered those around me in their not-as-comfortable seats. I invited several others I knew to join me in a better spot but was surprised they all wanted to stay in their own seats for various reasons: They didn't want to be inconvenienced with a move or felt fine where they were.

As believers in Christ, we have a much more significant invitation to extend: We've received a new life of faith in Jesus and want others to experience it too. Some will want to do so, and others won't. In John 1:40 we read that Andrew had begun to follow Jesus. The first thing Andrew did was to find his brother Simon and invite him to meet Jesus, the Messiah, too (v. 41). Jesus offered them a wonderful new way of life of knowing Him and enjoying His promises: His forgiveness (Romans 3:24), continual presence (Hebrews 13:5), hope (Romans 15:13), peace (John 14:27), and a forever future in His presence (1 Thessalonians 4:17).

Won't you join in? Jesus gives the best life.

—*Anne Cetas*

If you want someone to know what Christ will do for him, let him see what Christ has done for you.

X

HOPEFUL PRAISE

Read: Psalm 103:1-14

Praise the LORD, my soul, and forget not all his benefits.
—PSALM 103:2

One of my friends was in tears on a beautiful summer day, unable to deal with life's difficulties. Another could not look beyond the life-altering sadnesses of her past. Still another struggled with the closing of the small church he had pastored faithfully. A fourth friend had lost his job at a local ministry.

What can our struggling friends—or any of us—do to find hope? Where do we turn when tomorrow offers no happy promises?

We can praise or "bless" the Lord, as David said in Psalm 103. In the middle of trouble, acknowledging God's role in our lives can redirect our thinking from the hurts of our hearts and force us to dwell instead on the greatness of our God. David knew trouble. He faced the threat of enemies, the consequences of his own sin, and the challenges of sorrow. Yet he also recognized the healing power of praise.

That's why in Psalm 103 he can list reasons to turn our attention to God, who gives us many benefits: He forgives us, heals us, redeems us, crowns us with love and compassion, satisfies our desires, and renews us. David reminds us that God provides justice and righteousness and is gracious and loving.

Take it from David: Praising God's greatness puts hope in our troubled hearts.

—*Dave Branon*

Praise can lighten your heaviest burden.

HOPE FOR SKEPTICS

Read: Isaiah 55:6-13

So is my word that goes out from my mouth: It will not return to me empty.
—ISAIAH 55:11

As a workplace chaplain, I'm privileged to be able to talk with many different people. Some are skeptics of the Christian faith. I've discovered three major hurdles that keep them from trusting in Christ for salvation.

The first barrier, surprisingly, isn't an unwillingness to believe that God exists; instead some doubt that they're important enough for God's attention. Second, some believe they are unworthy of His forgiveness. People are often their own harshest judges. The third hurdle? They wonder why God is not communicating with them if He is out there.

Let's work backward through the hurdles to see what God's Word says. First, God doesn't play head games. He promises that if we read His Word, He will make sure it accomplishes His purpose (Isaiah 55:11). In other words, if we read it we will discover that God is communicating with us. This is precisely why the Bible speaks so often of His grace and mercy toward all (v. 7). His willingness to forgive surpasses our own. Once we learn that we can hear God in the Bible and once we see the emphasis on His mercy, it becomes easier to believe we have His attention when we cry out to Him.

God's story is amazing. It can give hope for all of us.

—*Randy Kilgore*

Honest skepticism can be the first step to a strong faith.

THE WARMTH OF THE SUN

Read: Psalm 6

I am worn out from my groaning. All night long I flood my bed
with weeping and drench my couch with tears. —PSALM 6:6

On a November day in 1963, Brian Wilson and Mike Love of the Beach Boys wrote a song quite unlike the band's typically upbeat tunes. It was a mournful song about love that's been lost. Mike said later, "As hard as that kind of loss is, the one good that comes from it is having had the experience of being in love in the first place." They titled it "The Warmth of the Sun."

Sorrow serving as a catalyst for songwriting is nothing new. Some of David's most moving psalms were penned in times of deep personal loss, including Psalm 6. Though we aren't told the events that prompted its writing, the lyrics are filled with grief, "I am worn out from my groaning. All night long I flood my bed with weeping . . . . My eyes grow weak with sorrow" (vv. 6–7).

But that's not where the song ends. David knew pain and loss, but he also knew God's comfort. So he wrote, "The LORD has heard my cry for mercy; the LORD accepts my prayer" (v. 9).

In his grief, David not only found a song but he also found reason to trust God, whose faithfulness bridges all of life's hard seasons. In the warmth of His presence, our sorrows gain a hopeful perspective.

—*Bill Crowder*

A song of sadness can turn our hearts to the God whose joy for us is forever.

GIVING IT TO GOD

Read: Mark 10:17-22

He went away sad, because he had great wealth. —MARK 10:22

A hero to a generation of people who grew up after World War II, Corrie ten Boom left a legacy of godliness and wisdom. A victim of the Nazi occupation of the Netherlands, she survived to tell her story of faith and dependence on God during horrendous suffering.

"I have held many things in my hands," Corrie once said, quoting a line attributed to Martin Luther, "and I have lost them all; but whatever I have placed in God's hands, that I still possess."

Corrie was well acquainted with loss. She lost family, possessions, and years of her life to hateful people. Yet she learned to concentrate on what could be gained spiritually and emotionally by putting everything in the hands of her heavenly Father.

What does that mean to us? What should we place in God's hands for safekeeping? According to the story of the rich young man in Mark 10: everything. He held abundance in his hands, but when Jesus asked him to give it up, he refused. He kept his possessions, but he failed to follow Jesus—and as a result he "went away sad" (v. 22).

Like Corrie ten Boom, we can find hope by putting everything in God's hands and then trusting Him for the outcome.

—*Dave Branon*

No life is more secure than a life surrendered to God.

UNCERTAIN TIMES

Read: Philippians 4:6-9

The peace of God, which transcends all understanding, will guard your hearts and your minds in Christ Jesus. —PHILIPPIANS 4:7

During a major economic downturn several years ago, many people lost their jobs. Sadly, my brother-in-law was one of them. Writing to me about their situation, my sister shared that although there were uncertainties, they had peace because they knew that God would care for them.

Believers in Jesus can have peace in the midst of uncertainties because we have the assurance that our heavenly Father loves us and cares for our needs (Matthew 6:25–34). We can bring all our concerns to Him with an attitude of thankfulness, trusting Him to meet our needs and give us peace (Philippians 4:6–7).

"The peace of God, which transcends all understanding," writes the apostle Paul, "will guard your hearts and your minds in Christ Jesus" (v. 7). To say the peace of God transcends all understanding reveals that we can't explain it, but we can experience it as He guards our hearts and minds.

Our peace comes from the confidence that the Lord loves us and He is in control. He alone provides the comfort that settles our nerves, fills our minds with hope, and allows us to relax even in the midst of changes and challenges.

—*Poh Fang Chia*

You will keep in perfect peace those whose minds are steadfast, because they trust in you. —Isaiah 26:3

))((

THE BEST THINGS IN LIFE

Read: Proverbs 23:1-18

Do not wear yourself out to get rich. —PROVERBS 23:4

An old adage says, "The best things in life are free." There's a lot of truth in that. Some people, however, believe that the best things in life are expensive or perhaps elusive. Recently I saw a sign that made me smile and think. It said, "The best things in life are not things." What a great way to say it! The value of family, friends, and faith points us to the realization that what matters most in life is all wrapped up in people and the Lord.

Solomon was well qualified to speak about material things because he "was greater in riches and wisdom than all the other kings of the earth" (1 Kings 10:23). His advice? "Do not wear yourself out to get rich; do not trust in your own cleverness. Cast but a glance at riches, and they are gone, for they will surely sprout wings and fly off to the sky" (Proverbs 23:4–5). His recommended course of action was, "Apply your heart to instruction and your ears to words of knowledge. . . . There is surely a future hope for you, and your hope will not be cut off" (vv. 12, 18).

The best things in life are the eternal riches that come from God's goodness and grace in Jesus Christ. We do not hold them in our hands but in our hearts.

—*David McCasland*

———

Our greatest riches are the riches we have in Christ.

THE LIGHTHOUSE

Read: Isaiah 61:1-6

*[The Lord bestows] on them a crown of beauty instead of ashes,
the oil of joy instead of mourning.* —ISAIAH 61:3

By its very existence, a ministry center in Huye, Rwanda, called the Lighthouse symbolizes redemption. It sits on land where, during the genocide in 1994, the country's president owned a grand home. This new structure, however, has been built by Christians as a beacon of light and hope. Housed there is a Bible institute where the goal is to raise up a new generation of Christian leaders. Also, there is a hotel, a restaurant, and other services for the community. Out of the "ashes" has come new life. Those who built the Lighthouse look to Jesus as their source of hope and redemption.

When Jesus went to the synagogue in Nazareth on the Sabbath, He read from the book of Isaiah and announced that He was the Anointed One to proclaim the Lord's favor (see Luke 4:14–21). He was the One who came to bind up the broken-hearted and offer redemption and forgiveness. In Jesus we see beauty coming from the ashes (Isaiah 61:3).

We find the atrocities of the Rwandan genocide, when intertribal fighting cost more than a half million lives, mind-boggling and harrowing. We hardly know what to say about them. Yet we know that the Lord can redeem the atrocities—either here on earth or in heaven. He who bestows the oil of joy instead of mourning gives us hope even in the midst of the darkest of situations.

—*Amy Boucher Pye*

Jesus came to bring us hope in the darkest of circumstances.

FAST FEET

Read: Philippians 4:10-19

The Sovereign LORD is my strength; he makes my feet like the feet of a deer, he enables me to tread on the heights. —HABAKKUK 3:19

While in Chile for a Bible conference, I was resting at the hotel when a rugby match came on the television. Though I don't fully understand rugby, I enjoy it and admire the courage it takes to play such a dangerous sport.

During the match, one of the French players was injured and had to be taken to the sidelines. As the trainers attended to him, the camera showed a closeup of his shoes. With a black marker the player had written the words: "Habakkuk 3:19" and "Jesus is the way." Those expressions of faith and hope were a strong testimony of that young athlete's priorities and values.

The verse cited on that rugby player's shoes is not just one of heavenly hope and persevering faith. It is one of practical value—especially to an athlete dependent on speed for success. It says, "The Sovereign LORD is my strength; he makes my feet like the feet of a deer, he enables me to tread on the heights."

In all of life, we need the strength and supply of our God. He alone can give us "feet" that are swift and strong. He alone can equip us for all of the uncertainties of life, for He alone is our strength. With Paul, we can be assured: "My God will meet all your needs" (Philippians 4:19).

—*Bill Crowder*

———

We always have enough when God is our supply.

A LIVING HOPE

Read: 1 Peter 1:3-9

Praise be to [God] . . . ! In his great mercy he has given us new birth into a living hope. —1 PETER 1:3

Life is hard for everybody, but it's much harder for some than for others. Putting our trust in Christ as our Savior does little to change that. Nothing in the Bible promises us a free pass merely because we are Christ's followers. In fact, some of our wounds may not heal and some of our deficiencies may not be corrected during our lifetime. They may even get worse. Yet our deformities and weaknesses are only temporary.

Anticipating what God has in store for us can put a smile in our heart. Hope gives us poise and lets us live with inner strength, because we know that one day we will be dramatically different than we are now.

If you are in some way damaged by past abuse or feeling defeated by sin, or if you feel so inferior to others that you walk with your eyes to the ground, take heart in what God has in store for you. Live today with the courage God gives you. Make what you can of your afflictions. But rejoice, because everything that degrades and limits you is only temporary. It will be gone—some of it sooner rather than later.

If you have a living hope in Christ, you can deal with your past because of your future. God's glorious best for you lies ahead.

—Haddon Robinson

Christians can cope with their past because they have hope for the future.

HOPE FOR WORRIERS

Read: Psalm 23

The LORD is my shepherd, I lack nothing. —PSALM 23:1

Everyone worries occasionally, but I was once a "professional worrier." My daily preoccupation was mulling over my worries, one by one.

Then one day I had to face an uncomfortable medical test, and I was frantic with fear. Finally, I decided that during the test I would focus on the first five words of Psalm 23, "The LORD is my shepherd." This exercise in meditation not only calmed me but it also helped me gain several fresh insights. Later, as I slowly meditated through the entire psalm, the Lord gave me more insights. Eventually I was able to share at conferences what the Lord had taught me.

If you're a worrier, there's hope for you too! Rick Warren, author of *The Purpose Driven Life*, wrote: "When you think about a problem over and over in your mind, that's called worry. When you think about God's Word over and over in your mind, that's meditation. If you know how to worry, you already know how to meditate!"

The more we meditate on God's Word, the less we need to worry. In Psalm 23, David meditated on his great Shepherd instead of worrying. Later, God chose him to be the shepherd of His people (Psalm 78:70–72). God uses those who can honestly say, "The Lord is my shepherd."

—*Joanie Yoder*

The more we think about God's Word, the less we'll think about our worries.

)X(

HOPE LIVES

Read: 1 Peter 1:3-9

Your faith—of greater worth than gold . . . may result in praise, glory and honor when Jesus Christ is revealed. —1 PETER 1:7

When unspeakable tragedy shatters people's lives, they search for answers. Recently, a mother who had lost a teenager said to me, "I can't figure it out. I don't know if I can believe anymore. I try, but God doesn't make sense to me. What does it all mean?" There are no easy answers to such big concerns. But for those who have trusted Christ, there is hope—whether we are basking in blessings or grinding through grief.

Peter spells this out in his first letter. In glowing terms, he praises God for our "new birth into a living hope" (1 Peter 1:3) through our salvation. That hope can bring joy even in the middle of tragedy. He also assures us of the permanence of this hope (v. 4). He then tells us of the heart-breaking reality that we may "suffer grief in all kinds of trials" (v. 6). Those who have suffered loss turn hopeful hearts toward Peter's next words: These come so that "your faith . . . may result in praise, glory and honor when Jesus Christ is revealed" (v. 7).

Trials—seemingly random and inexplicable—can be seen differently in the light of these words. In the midst of tragedy, the power and beauty of our salvation can shine through because of our great Savior. And that may be just enough light to get a troubled person through another day.

—*Dave Branon*

————

The light of salvation shines clearly even in the darkest night.

EVERYTHING IS BEAUTIFUL

Read: Joel 2:18-27

I will repay you for the years the locusts have eaten. —JOEL 2:25

The beauty of the black lacy design against the pastel purple and orange background grabbed my attention. The intricacy of the fragile pattern led me to assume that it had been created by a skilled artist. As I looked more closely at the photo, however, I saw the artist admiring his work from a corner of the photo. The "artist" was a worm, and its work of art was a partially eaten leaf.

What made the image beautiful was not the destruction of the leaf but the light glowing through the holes. As I gazed at the photo, I began thinking about lives that have been eaten by the "worms" of sin. The effects are ravaging. Sin eats away at us as we suffer the consequences of our own bad choices or those of others. We are all its victims.

But the photo also reminded me of the hope we have in God. Through the prophet Joel, God said to Israel, "I will repay you for the years the locusts have eaten" (Joel 2:25). And from Isaiah we learn that the Lord appointed him to "comfort all who mourn, and provide for those who grieve in Zion—to bestow on them a crown of beauty" (Isaiah 61:3 NKJV).

Satan does everything he can to make us ugly, but despite our enemy's best efforts, the Light of the World can restore us and make us beautiful.

—*Julie Ackerman Link*

Sins are like weeds in a garden; we must pull them out or they will take over.

LONG-AWAITED REUNION

Read: 1 Thessalonians 4:13–18

We who are still alive and are left will be caught up together
with them in the clouds to meet the Lord in the air.
—1 THESSALONIANS 4:17

As a boy, I had a collie named Prince Boy, a great dog that I really loved. One day, he disappeared. I didn't know if he had been stolen or if he had simply run away—but I was devastated. I searched everywhere. In fact, one of my earliest childhood memories is of climbing a tall tree from which I could scan our neighborhood in hopes of spotting him. I desperately wanted my beloved dog back. For weeks, I was always watching and hoping to see Prince Boy again. But we were never reunited.

There's a much greater sense of loss when we think we'll never again see a loved one who dies. But for those who know and love the Lord, death's parting is only temporary. One day we will be reunited forever!

Paul assured the Thessalonians, "The dead in Christ will rise first. After that, we who are still alive and are left will be caught up together with them in the clouds to meet the Lord in the air. And so we will be with the Lord forever" (1 Thessalonians 4:16–17). The words that provide comfort to the grieving heart are *together* and *we*. These words of reunion indicate that followers of Christ don't ever have to experience permanent separation. For us, death is not a goodbye; it's a "see you later."

—*Bill Crowder*

God's people never say goodbye for the last time.

HOPE FOR A MUDDER

Read: James 1:2-4

Suffering produces perseverance; perseverance, character;
and character, hope. —ROMANS 5:3–4

When my husband built a covered porch on the front of our house, he anticipated that someday a bird might try to build a nest there. So he built the top of the corner post on a slant. Later we laughed smugly when we saw robins trying their best to claim squatting rights to a new home. Piles of grass on the porch revealed their wasted efforts. But after two days of steady rain, we saw that a nest had indeed appeared in the very spot we thought was impossible. Because of the rain, Mrs. Robin was able to mix up a batch of mud mortar. Weaving it with twigs and grass, our determined feathered friend had built herself a new nest. She had persevered.

Perseverance is inspiring! Trying to live a Christ-honoring life while experiencing hardship can leave us frustrated and discouraged. But when we depend on God to help us through our difficulties, we are empowered to keep going even when we can't always see the resolution of our problems. Galatians 6:9 reminds us not to "become weary in doing good" and encourages us not to give up.

Is our loving God using a seemingly insurmountable challenge in your life to produce perseverance? Let Him produce in you character—and through character, hope (Romans 5:3–4).

—*Cindy Hess Kasper*

———

When the world says, "Give up," hope whispers, "Try it one more time!"

AWAKENED BY
A CLOSE FRIEND

Read: John 14:1-7

You also may be where I am. —JOHN 14:3

A few years ago I had some tests to screen for cancer, and I was nervous about the outcome. My anxiety was magnified as I thought about the fact that while the medical personnel were well trained and extremely competent, they were also strangers who had no relationship with me.

After awakening from the anesthesia, however, I heard the beautiful sound of my wife's voice: "It's great, Honey. They didn't find anything." I looked up at her smiling face and was comforted. I needed the assurance of someone who loved me.

A similar assurance lies ahead for all who have trusted Jesus. Believers can be comforted in knowing that when they wake up in heaven, One who loves them greatly—Jesus—will be there.

The Book of Common Prayer expresses this Christian hope: "After my awakening, [my Redeemer] will raise me up; and in my body I shall see God. I myself shall see, and eyes behold Him who is my friend and not a stranger."

Do you have trouble facing mortality? Jesus promised to be there when we slip from this world into the next. He said, "Where I am [heaven], there you may be also" (John 14:3 NKJV). What a comfort for us as believers to know that after death we will be awakened by a close Friend!

—*Dennis Fisher*

To see Jesus will be heaven's greatest joy.

✕

NO HOPE BUT GOD

Read: Romans 5:1-5

If we hope for what we do not yet have, we wait for it patiently.
—ROMANS 8:25

In his book *Through the Valley of the Kwai*, Scottish officer Ernest Gordon wrote of his years as a prisoner of war (POW) during World War II. This 6' 2" man suffered from malaria, diphtheria, typhoid, beriberi, dysentery, and jungle ulcers; and the hard labor and scarcity of food quickly plunged his weight to less than one hundred pounds.

The squalor of the prison hospital prompted a desperate Ernest to request to be moved to a cleaner place—the morgue. Lying in the dirt of the death house, he waited to die. But every day, a fellow prisoner came to wash his wounds and to encourage him to eat part of his own rations. As the quiet and unassuming Dusty Miller nursed Ernest back to health, he talked with the agnostic Scotsman of his own strong faith in God and showed him that—even in the midst of suffering—there is hope.

The hope we read about in Scripture is not a vague, wishy-washy optimism. Instead, biblical hope is a strong and confident expectation that what God has promised in His Word He will accomplish. Tribulation is often the catalyst that produces perseverance, character, and finally, hope (Romans 5:3–4).

More than seventy years ago, in a brutal POW camp, Ernest Gordon learned this truth himself and said, "Faith thrives when there is no hope but God" (see Romans 8:24–25).

—*Cindy Hess Kasper*

Christ, the Rock, is our sure hope.

SONRISE

Read: Malachi 4:1-6

The sun of righteousness will rise with healing in its rays.
—MALACHI 4:2

My state's name, "Idaho," according to one legend, comes from a Shoshone Indian word, "ee-dah-how." When translated into English, it means something like, "Behold! The sun rising over the mountain." I often think of that when the sun breaks over the eastern peaks and spills light and life into our valley.

Also, I think of Malachi's promise: "The sun of righteousness will rise with healing in its rays" (Malachi 4:2). This is God's irrevocable promise that our Lord Jesus will come again and all creation "will be liberated from its bondage to decay and brought into the freedom and glory of the children of God" (Romans 8:21).

Each new sunrise is a reminder of that eternal morning when "the sun of righteousness" will arise with healing in His wings. Then everything that has been made will be made over and made irrevocably right. There will be no throbbing backs or knees, no financial struggles, no losses, no aging. Malachi says that when Jesus returns we will "go out and frolic like well-fed calves" (4:2). This is my highest imagination and my hope.

Jesus said, "Yes, I am coming soon" (Revelation 22:20). Even so, come, Lord Jesus!

—*David Roper*

—

You have reason for optimism if you're looking for Christ's return.

HOPE IN HIM

Read: Isaiah 53

The virgin will conceive and give birth to a son,
and will call him Immanuel. —ISAIAH 7:14

As we drove home from a Christmas party one evening, my family and I approached a small country church nestled between glittering snowbanks. From a distance, I could see its holiday display. Strings of white lights formed the capital letters: H-O-P-E. The sight of that word shining in the darkness reminded me that Jesus is, and always has been, the hope of humankind.

Before Jesus was born, people hoped for the Messiah—the One who would shoulder their sin and intercede with God on their behalf (Isaiah 53:12). They expected the Messiah to arrive through a virgin who would bear a son in Bethlehem and would name Him Immanuel (7:14), which means, "God with us." The night Jesus was born, their hope was fulfilled (Luke 2:1–14).

Although we're no longer waiting for Jesus in the form of an infant, He is still the source of our hope. We watch for His second coming (Matthew 24:30), we anticipate the heavenly home He is preparing for us (John 14:2), and we dream of living with Him in His celestial city (1 Thessalonians 4:16). As Christians, we can look forward to the future because the baby in the manger was, and still is, "Christ Jesus our hope" (1 Timothy 1:1).

—*Jennifer Benson Schuldt*

The key word of Christmas is "Immanuel"—God with us!

FALSE HOPE

Read: Ephesians 2:1-10

For it is by grace you have been saved, through faith—and this is not
from yourselves, it is the gift of God—not by works.
—EPHESIANS 2:8–9

The name of a pretty Bavarian town in Germany shares the name of a place of horror—Dachau. A museum on the grounds of this infamous Nazi concentration camp attracts many World War II history buffs.

As you look around, it would be hard to miss the misleading words welded to an iron gate: "Arbeit Macht Frei." This phrase—"Work Makes You Free"—was just a cruel lie to give false hope to those who entered this place of death.

Many people today have false hope that they can earn a place in heaven by working at being good or by doing good things. God's standard of perfection, however, requires a totally sinless life. There's no way any of us can ever be "good enough." It is only through the sacrifice of the sinless Savior that we are made righteous. God made Jesus "who had no sin to be sin for us, so that in him we might become the righteousness of God" (2 Corinthians 5:21). Eternal life is given because of God's gift of grace—not because of our good works (Ephesians 2:8–9).

Don't let Satan trick you by giving you false hope that your good works will save you. It is only through Jesus's work on the cross that you can have real freedom.

—*Cindy Hess Kasper*

We are not saved by good works but by God's work.

THE RIGHT INFORMATION

Read: 1 Thessalonians 4:13-18

Brothers and sisters, we do not want you to be uninformed about those who sleep in death, so that you do not grieve like the rest of mankind, who have no hope. —1 THESSALONIANS 4:13

Our flight had been airborne about fifteen minutes when the pilot announced that the aircraft had a serious problem the crew was trying to analyze. A few minutes later, he announced that it was a vibration and that we would have to return to the airport. Then the flight attendants made a series of step-by-step announcements explaining what was going on and what would happen once we were on the ground. In an event that could have been terrifying, the fears of the passengers were relieved because we were given the right information.

In the first century, a group of believers in Thessalonica were afraid that their believing loved ones who had died were gone forever and would miss out on the second coming of Christ. For that reason, Paul wrote, "we do not want you to be uninformed about those who sleep in death, so that you do not grieve like the rest of mankind, who have no hope" (1 Thessalonians 4:13). Paul's words of comfort were intended to soften their fears by giving them the right information, which made all the difference in the world. While grieving their loss, they could still have hope of a coming reunion with those who were in Christ.

In seasons of loss, we too can find comfort and hope because the Bible has given us the right information.

—*Bill Crowder*

Death is not a period—it's only a comma.

ХⅩ

SHORT-TIMERS

Read: Romans 5:1-5

Hope does not disappoint. —ROMANS 5:5 NKJV

I served in the Armed Forces many years ago and have always been thankful that I was able to give those years to my country. I must say, however, that my most memorable time in the service was the brief interval when I was a "short-timer."

Short-timers are soldiers who have but a few weeks before discharge. They spend their last days "mustering out"—visiting the commissary and the quartermaster's office to clear accounts and return equipment. What I remember most about that period was my jaunty pace and the happy, carefree spirit with which I carried out my tasks. I had duties but few worries, for I knew I was going home.

Now that I'm an "old-timer," once again I'm a short-timer. It won't be long before I'm discharged from my duty here. Again, my pace is jaunty and my spirit is light for I know that very soon I'll be going home. That's the outlook that Jesus and His apostles called "hope" (Acts 24:15; Romans 5:2, 5).

Hope, in the biblical sense, means "certainty and assurance." It is the firm, unshakable, indomitable belief that we will be raised from the dead (as Jesus was) and will be welcomed into our eternal home. That's enough to put joy in our heart and a spring in our step this day!

—*David Roper*

The risen Christ will come from heaven to take His own to heaven.

A LITTLE PIECE OF HEAVEN

Read: Exodus 25:1-9

Don't you know that you yourselves are God's temple and that God's Spirit dwells in your midst? —1 CORINTHIANS 3:16

One day not long ago, my wife met a woman who needed a ride. She sensed that this could be from God, so she agreed to take her to her destination. During the ride, the woman revealed to my wife that she was a believer, but she struggled with drug addiction. My wife listened to and talked with this hurting woman. As she gave her hope for a better tomorrow, I believe that in some small way the woman experienced a little piece of heaven on earth.

When God instructed Moses to build the tabernacle according to His specifications, it was so that God's people would sense His presence. I like to think of it as a little piece of heaven on earth. The temple was a physical example of God's presence on earth also (1 Kings 5–8). The purpose of these holy places was for God to dwell among His people. This was God's plan when Jesus, the perfect temple, "made his dwelling among us" (John 1:14).

When Jesus ascended to heaven, He sent the Holy Spirit to indwell His followers (John 14:16–17), so we would be God's tabernacles and temples in the world (1 Corinthians 3:16; 6:19). As God's representatives of His presence, let's find ways to bring the peace and hope of heaven to others on earth.

—*Marvin Williams*

A Christian who is willing to do little things for others can do great things for the Lord.

FINDING HOPE

Read: Psalm 42:1-11

*Why, my soul, are you downcast? . . . Put your hope in God,
for I will yet praise him.* —PSALM 42:5

A study conducted by researchers at the University of Minnesota found that almost fifteen percent of American teenagers felt it was "highly likely" that they would die before their thirty-fifth birthday. Those with this pessimistic outlook were more likely to engage in reckless behavior. Dr. Iris Borowsky, author of the study published in the journal *Pediatrics*, said, "These youth may take risks because they feel hopeless and figure that not much is at stake."

No one is immune to feelings of despair. The Psalms express repeated pleas for help when life seems dark. "Why are you in despair, O my soul? And why have you become disturbed within me? Hope in God, for I shall again praise Him for the help of His presence" (Psalm 42:5 NASB). In a defiant step of faith, the psalmist tells himself not to forget about God, who will never forsake him.

Curtis Almquist has written: "Hope is fueled by the presence of God. . . . [It] is also fueled by the future of God in our lives." We can say with the psalmist, "I will yet praise him" (v. 5).

No follower of Christ should feel reluctant to seek counsel for depression. Nor should we feel that faith and prayer are too simplistic to help. There is always hope in God!

—*David McCasland*

Hope for the Christian is a certainty—because its basis is Christ.

SO LONG

Read: 1 Thessalonians 4:13-18

Do not grieve like the rest of mankind, who have no hope.
—1 THESSALONIANS 4:13

My grandfather refused to say "goodbye." He felt the word was too final. So when we would drive away after family visits, his farewell ritual was always the same. Standing in front of the green ferns that lined his house, he would wave and call out, "So long!"

As believers, we never have to say "goodbye" to the ones we love, as long as they have placed their trust in Jesus as Savior. The Bible promises that we will see them again.

The apostle Paul said that we should not "grieve like the rest of mankind, who have no hope" (1 Thessalonians 4:13), because when Jesus returns, the Christians who have died will rise from their graves and—together with the believers who are still alive—will meet the Lord in the air (vv. 15–17). We have confidence that one day in heaven there will be "no more death or mourning or crying" (Revelation 21:4). It's in that wonderful place that "we will be with the Lord forever" (1 Thessalonians 4:17).

Christians have the hope of an eternal reunion with Christ and with believing loved ones who have passed away. That's why Paul exhorted us to "encourage one another with these words" (v.18). Today, encourage someone with the hope that allows us to say "so long" instead of "goodbye."

—*Jennifer Benson Schuldt*

———

At death, God's people don't say "Goodbye," but "We'll see you later."

A WORD TO THE WEARY

Read: Isaiah 50:4-10

The Sovereign Lord has given me a well-instructed tongue to know the word that sustains the weary. —ISAIAH 50:4

The people of Israel were struggling. They had been taken captive by the Assyrians and forced to live in a country far from home. What could the prophet Isaiah give these weary people to help them?

He gave them a prophecy of hope. It was a message from God relating to the promised Messiah. In Isaiah 50:4, the Savior himself described the comfort and consolation He would one day bring: "The Sovereign Lord has given me a well-instructed tongue to know the word that sustains the weary."

These were words of dual comfort—both to the people in exile and to future generations whose lives would be touched by Jesus's compassion. In the Gospels we see how Christ fulfilled the prophecy with "a word in season to him who is weary" (Isaiah 50:4). To the crowds who followed Him, Christ proclaimed: "Come to me, all you who are weary and burdened, and I will give you rest" (Matthew 11:28). Words of compassion indeed!

Jesus left us an example of how to minister to people who have grown weary. Do you know someone who needs a timely word of encouragement or the listening ear of a concerned friend? A word of comfort to the weary can go a long way.

—*Dennis Fisher*

Compassion is needed to heal
the hurts of others.

𝄡

SEEING TO TOMORROW

Read: 2 Corinthians 5:1-9

We live by faith, not by sight. —2 CORINTHIANS 5:7

I enjoy gazing up at a cloudless blue sky. The sky is a beautiful part of our great Creator's masterpiece, given for us to enjoy. Imagine how much pilots must love the view. They use several aeronautical terms to describe a perfect sky for flying, but my favorite is, "You can see to tomorrow."

"Seeing to tomorrow" is beyond our view. Sometimes we even struggle to see or understand what life is throwing at us today. The Bible tells us, "Why, you do not even know what will happen tomorrow. What is your life? You are a mist that appears for a little while and then vanishes" (James 4:14).

But our limited visibility is not cause for despair. Just the opposite. We trust in the God who sees all of our tomorrows perfectly—and who knows what we need as we face the challenges ahead. The apostle Paul knew this. That's why Paul encourages us with hopeful words: "We live by faith, not by sight" (2 Corinthians 5:7).

When we trust God with our day as well as our unseen tomorrows, we don't need to worry about anything life throws at us. We walk with Him and He knows what is ahead; He is strong enough and wise enough to handle it.

—*Bill Crowder*

God sees the beginning to the end.

A SECOND CHANCE

Read: Lamentations 3:22-33

His compassions never fail. They are new every morning; great is your faithfulness. —LAMENTATIONS 3:22–23

On January 15, 2009, 155 people on US Airways Flight 1549 thought they were going to die. During takeoff from New York City, their plane struck a flock of geese, disabling both engines. In a powerless glide, the captain maneuvered over the densely populated area, then announced: "Brace for impact." Less than ninety seconds later, the crippled plane made a water landing in the frigid Hudson River, where boats and ferries quickly arrived to rescue the passengers and crew, all of whom survived. People called it the "miracle on the Hudson" and praised the pilot and crew. One grateful passenger said simply, "We have a second chance in life."

In times of crisis, we grasp the importance of every hour. During our ordinary routine, however, we often forget that each day is a second chance. "Because of the LORD's great love we are not consumed, for his compassions never fail. They are new every morning; great is your faithfulness. I say to myself, 'The LORD is my portion; therefore I will wait for him'" (Lamentations 3:22–24).

We can choose to live with thankfulness for God's mercy and grace, with confidence in His faithful care, and with hope because He is with us forever. Today, God offers us a second chance in life. Let's make the most of it!

—*David McCasland*

Our God is a God of second chances.

NOTHING LEFT BUT GOD

Read: 2 Chronicles 20:3-17

Do not be afraid or discouraged because of this vast army. For the battle is not yours, but God's. —2 CHRONICLES 20:15

A wise Bible teacher once said, "Sooner or later God will bring self-sufficient people to the place where they have no resource but Him—no strength, no answers, nothing but Him. Without God's help, they're sunk."

He then told of a despairing man who confessed to his pastor, "My life is really in bad shape." "How bad?" the pastor inquired. Burying his head in his hands, he moaned, "I'll tell you how bad—all I've got left is God." The pastor's face lit up. "I'm happy to assure you that a person with nothing left but God has more than enough for great victory!"

In today's Bible reading, the people of Judah were also in trouble. They admitted their lack of power and wisdom to conquer their foes. All they had left was God! But King Jehoshaphat and the people saw this as reason for hope, not despair. "Our eyes are on you," they declared to God (2 Chronicles 20:12). And their hope was not disappointed as He fulfilled His promise: "The battle is not yours, but God's" (v. 15).

Are you in a position where all self-sufficiency is gone? As you turn your eyes on the Lord and put your hope in Him, you have God's reassuring promise that you need nothing more.

—*Joanie Yoder*

When all you have is God, you have all you need.

FLYING MACHINES

Read: Psalm 6

I am worn out from my groaning. All night long I flood my bed with weeping and drench my couch with tears. —PSALM 6:6

Recording artist James Taylor exploded onto the music scene in early 1970 with the song "Fire and Rain." In it, he talked about the disappointments of life, referring to them as flying machines that ended up in pieces on the ground. That was a reference to Taylor's original band Flying Machine, whose attempt at breaking into the recording industry had failed badly, causing him to wonder if his dreams of a musical career would ever come true. The reality of crushed expectations had taken their toll, leaving Taylor with a sense of loss and hopelessness.

The psalmist David also experienced hopeless despair as he struggled with his own failures, the attacks of others, and the disappointments of life. In Psalm 6:6 he said, "I am worn out from my groaning. All night long I flood my bed with weeping and drench my couch with tears." The depth of his sorrow and loss drove him to heartache—but in that grief he turned to the God of all comfort. David's own crushed and broken "flying machines" gave way to the assurance of God's care, prompting him to say, "The LORD has heard my cry for mercy; the LORD accepts my prayer" (v. 9).

In our own seasons of disappointment, we too can find comfort in God, who cares for our broken hearts.

—*Bill Crowder*

God's whisper of comfort quiets the noise of our trials.

THE GIFT OF WELCOME

Read: Hebrews 13:1-2

Do not forget to show hospitality to strangers.
—HEBREWS 13:2

The dinner we hosted for families from five nations remains a wonderful memory. Somehow the conversation didn't splinter into twos, but we all contributed to a discussion of life in London from the viewpoints of residents of different parts of the world. At the end of the evening, my husband and I reflected that we had received more than we gave, including the warm feelings we experienced in fostering new friendships and learning about different cultures.

The writer of the book of Hebrews concluded his thoughts with some exhortations for community life, including that his readers should continue to welcome strangers. For in doing so, "some people have shown hospitality to angels without knowing it" (13:2). He may have been referring to Abraham and Sarah, who welcomed three strangers, reaching out to them with generosity and treating them to a feast, as was the custom in biblical times (see Genesis 18:1–2). They didn't know that they were entertaining angels who brought them a message of blessing.

We don't ask people into our homes in the hope of gaining from them, but often we receive more than we give. May the Lord spread His love through us as we reach out with His welcome.

—*Amy Boucher Pye*

When we practice hospitality,
we share God's goodness and gifts.

)X(

HOPE THAT BANISHES HOPELESSNESS

Read: Philippians 2:5-11

May I never boast except in the cross of our Lord Jesus Christ.
—GALATIANS 6:14

When atheistic communism was a world-menacing power, it proclaimed that there is no God and that faith in any future life is a deceptive illusion. Leonid Brezhnev had been the Soviet dictator, the embodiment of Marxist unbelief. But something happened at his funeral that contradicted atheism. George H. W. Bush, then vice president of the US, was the country's official representative at the solemn, formal ceremony.

He reported that while the casket was still open, Brezhnev's widow stared motionless at her husband's body. Then, just before the soldiers were about to close the lid, she reached inside and made the sign of the cross over his chest. What a desperate and significant gesture! That widow evidently hoped that what her husband had vehemently denied might somehow be true.

Thankfully, we can have hope beyond this earthly life! All we need to do is embrace by faith the saving message of the cross: Jesus died for our sins and rose again so we might live eternally with Him. Do you believe? Then join with the apostle Paul in affirming that "we have put our hope in the living God, who is the Savior of all people, and especially of those who believe" (1 Timothy 4:10).

—*Vernon Grounds*

Calvary's cross is the only bridge to eternal life.

THE HOPE OF HEAVEN

Read: Psalm 71:9-18

My flesh and my heart may fail, but God is the strength of my heart and my portion forever. —PSALM 73:26

A woman in her eighties was bedridden in a nursing home. When a preacher came to visit her, she asked him the same question she had asked of other preachers: "Why am I here like this? I've been a Christian for years and have always served God. I taught Sunday school, sang in the choir, and brought up my children as Christians. Now look at me. Can you tell me why I'm here like this?" To her surprise, he answered, "Yes, I can." "Then tell me," she begged. He took her hand and said gently, "Old age."

I knew a Christian woman who also lived in a nursing home but accepted her old age. Although she experienced pain and weakness, she said, "In this corner I work for the Lord—and the Lord works on me!"

Psalm 71 tells us that there is still work to be done for God, even when health and strength fail. "I will always have hope" (v. 14). "My mouth will tell of your righteous deeds" (v. 15). "Since my youth, God, you have taught me, and to this day I declare your marvelous deeds" (v. 17).

And when your work on earth is done—what then? "You guide me . . . and afterward you will take me into glory" (73:24). Whatever your age, condition, or circumstances, if you're a Christian, the hope of heaven is yours!

—*Joanie Yoder*

As the years add up, God's faithfulness multiplies.

FOR THE WEARY

Read: Isaiah 40:27-31

Those who hope in the LORD will renew their strength.
—ISAIAH 40:31

On a beautiful, sunny day, I was walking in a park yet feeling very weary in spirit. It wasn't just one thing weighing me down—it seemed to be everything. When I stopped to sit on a bench, I noticed a small plaque placed there in loving memory of a "devoted husband, father, brother, and friend." Also on the plaque were these words, "But they who wait for the LORD shall renew their strength; they shall mount up with wings like eagles; they shall run and not be weary, they shall walk and not faint" (Isaiah 40:31 ESV).

Those familiar words came to me as a personal touch from the Lord. Weariness—whether physical, emotional, or spiritual—comes to us all. Isaiah reminds us that although we become tired, the Lord, the everlasting God, the Creator of the ends of the earth "will not grow tired or weary" (v. 28). How easily I had forgotten that in every situation "[the Lord] gives strength to the weary and increases the power of the weak" (v. 29).

What's it like on your journey today? If fatigue has caused you to forget God's presence and power, why not pause and recall His promise. "Those who hope in the Lord will renew their strength" (v. 31). Here. Now. Right where we are.

—*David McCasland*

When life's struggles make you weary, find strength in the Lord.

THE HOPE OF THE HEART

Read: Romans 4:13-15

He did not waver through unbelief regarding the promise of God,
but was strengthened in his faith and gave glory to God.
—ROMANS 4:20

Promises are the hope of our heart. A child's security depends on a parent's promise to keep him or her safe. A spouse can live with confidence because of a mate's promise of fidelity, loyalty, and love. Businesses depend on promises from employees, vendors, and clients. Countries remain safe when neighbors keep their promise to honor their borders.

Unfortunately, hearts and relationships are broken in all of those situations by unkept promises. There is one Promise-Maker, though, who can be trusted completely and without fear. That one is God. He has given us hundreds of promises in His Word, and He keeps every one of them.

If anyone had reason to wonder if God could or would keep His promises, it was Abraham. But "against all hope, Abraham in hope believed" (Romans 4:18). We know that what God had promised him—that he and his wife would have a child when they were both past ninety years old—could not have happened without divine intervention.

Are you looking for hope? Then search the Scriptures diligently and claim the promises of God that apply to you. Promises truly are the hope of the heart, and God always keeps His word.

—*Dave Branon*

The future always looks bright when viewed through the window of God's promises.

THE HEAVENLY ALTERNATIVE

Read: 2 Corinthians 5:1–11

*We are confident, I say, and would prefer to be away from the body
and at home with the Lord.* —2 CORINTHIANS 5:8

Recently, I wished a young friend "happy birthday" and asked
him how it felt to be a year older. His playful response? "Well,
I guess it's better than the alternative!"

We laughed together, but I later stopped to think—is it
really? Don't misunderstand me. I'm happy to live as long as
the Lord allows me to live and to watch my kids and grandkids
grow and experience life. I'm not excited about the inevitabil-
ity of death. But as a believer, the alternative to getting older is
heaven—and that's not bad!

In 2 Corinthians 5, Paul talks about the reality of living
with the aches and pains of our physical bodies, our "tents"
of flesh. But we should not live in despair about aging. In fact,
the apostle calls us to just the opposite. He wrote, "We are
confident, I say, and would prefer to be away from the body
and at home with the Lord" (v. 8). Confident! Pleased! Why?
Because our alternative to earthly life is that we will be present with the Lord—forever! The heavenly perspective of what
awaits us can give us confidence for living now.

If you know Christ, His promise can give you strength as
you go through today and bright hope as you look ahead to
tomorrow. What a great alternative!

—*Bill Crowder*

Death is gain because it means heaven, holiness, and Him!

)(

OUR ONLY HOPE

Read: 1 Thessalonians 4:13-18

We should live . . . godly in the present age, looking for the blessed hope.
—TITUS 2:12–13 NKJV

An anonymous author wrote, "When I was first converted, and for some years afterward, the second coming of Christ was a thrilling idea, a blessed hope, a glorious promise, the theme of some of the most inspiring songs of the church.

"Later it became an accepted tenet of faith, a cardinal doctrine, a kind of invisible trademark of my ministry. It was the favorite arena of my theological discussions, in the pulpit and in print. Now suddenly the second coming means something more to me. Paul called it 'the blessed hope.' But today it appears as the only hope of the world."

From the human standpoint, there is no solution for the struggles of the world. Leaders are naturally frustrated in trying to deal with the increasing problems in society. The only complete and permanent solution is found in the return of Christ to earth. When He comes, He will set up His kingdom. He will rule the nations in righteousness, and "the earth will be filled with the knowledge of the glory of the LORD as the waters cover the sea" (Habakkuk 2:14).

As we await our Savior's return, let us keep on praying, working, and watching, while "looking for the blessed hope"— our only hope for this world.

—*Richard DeHaan*

As this world gets darker, the promised return of God's Son gets brighter.

THE GOD OF VICTORY

Read: 2 Corinthians 2:14-17

Do not be overcome by evil, but overcome evil with good.
—ROMANS 12:21

In Greek mythology, Nike was the goddess of victory. Nike fought on the side of the Olympian gods, gaining a victory over the mighty Titans. As a result, she became a symbol of winning. But Nike's alleged powers were not just limited to warfare. She also became a favorite goddess of athletes who wanted to win in competitive sports. The Romans adopted her into their worship and gave her the Latin name Victoria.

In the Greco-Roman world where Paul taught, victory was highly valued. So when he expressed Christian truth, he used words his audience could understand. In his letters, he described Christ as the One who leads us in a military procession of triumph (2 Corinthians 2:14–17) and compared the Christian life to someone training for the ancient Olympic games (1 Corinthians 9:24–27).

Paul also used the word for victory in reference to our struggles with those who intentionally hurt us. "Overcome [be a victor over] evil with good" (Romans 12:21). This may mean returning kindness for spite or respectfully setting limits on evil behavior. In either case, an attitude of love cannot be generated in our own strength. But in Christ, we have divine power that ancient pagans could only hope for. Jesus Christ is the genuine God of victory.

—Dennis Fisher

———

God will give us the victory when we join Him in the fight.

HOPE FOR THE BLUES

Read: Psalm 62

Pour out your heart to him, for God is our refuge. —PSALM 62:8

You've felt it yourself, or at least listened to other people talk about it—the blues, times of dark discouragement. Lynette Hoy, in an article for christianwomentoday.com, tells of several steps we can take during those dark times to turn toward Jesus, the Light of the World:

Light up your heart through prayer. Pour out your heart to God when you're feeling overwhelmed (Psalm 62:8). Take your anxieties to Him in prayer (Philippians 4:6–7). And if you journal or write down your prayers, you can look back later to see how the Lord has answered you.

Light up your mind with truth. Read the Word of God every day, at least for a few minutes. Let His truth challenge, permeate, and transform your incorrect thinking that life is hopeless (Psalm 46:1; Romans 12:2).

Light up your life by doing God's will. His will for you is to worship and serve Him. Stay involved in your church where you can worship and fellowship with others and serve Him (Hebrews 10:25). This will help you grow in your trust of God.

When we feel darkness begin to close in on us, we need to turn to Jesus, the Light. He will be a refuge (Psalm 62:7–8) and will give us the strength to keep going.

—*Anne Cetas*

You won't stumble in the dark if you walk in the light of God's Word.

VICTORY OVER DEATH!

Read: John 5:24-30

A time is coming when all who are in their graves will hear his voice and come out. —JOHN 5:28–29

An ancient painting I recently saw made a deep impression on me. Its title, *Anastasis*, means "resurrection," and the painting depicts in a stunning way the triumph of Christ's victory over death. The Lord Jesus, newly emerged from the tomb, is pulling Adam and Eve out of their coffins and into eternal life. What is so amazing about this artwork is the way it shows how spiritual and physical death, the result of the fall, are dramatically reversed by the risen Christ.

Prior to His death on the cross, the Lord Jesus predicted a future day when He will call believers into a new and glorified existence: "A time is coming when all who are in their graves will hear His voice and come out" (John 5:28–29).

Because of Christ's victory over death, the grave is not final. We naturally will feel sorrow and grief when those we love die, and we are separated from them in this life. But the believer does not grieve as one who has no hope (1 Thessalonians 4:13). The witness of Jesus's resurrection is that all Christians will one day be taken from their graves to be clothed with glorified resurrection bodies (1 Corinthians 15:42–44). And so "we will be with the Lord forever" (1 Thessalonians 4:17).

—*Dennis Fisher*

Because Christ is alive, we too shall live.

HOPES AND DREAMS

Read: Acts 20:16-24

My only aim is to finish the race and complete the task the Lord Jesus has given me—the task of testifying to the good news of God's grace.
—ACTS 20:24

In 1960, everyone in the high school I attended participated in Project Talent. For several days, we took tests that surveyed our aptitudes in academic subjects. In addition, we were asked to express our plans, hopes, and dreams for the future. What we didn't know was that we were among 400,000 participants from 1,300 schools in the largest study of high school students ever conducted in the US. None of us involved in the study could have imagined how our lives would turn out.

The same was true for Saul of Tarsus. As a young man, his goal was to destroy the followers of Jesus (Acts 7:58–8:3; Galatians 1:13). But after his conversion, he became the apostle Paul, whose mission was to multiply them. As he journeyed to Jerusalem, facing prison and hardship, Paul said, "I consider my life worth nothing to me; my only aim is to finish the race and complete the task the Lord Jesus has given me—the task of testifying to the good news of God's grace" (Acts 20:24).

When our goal is to honor the Lord, He guides and guards us each step of the way. Whatever our hopes and dreams may be, when we place them in God's hands we know that everything, including setback or success, is under His control.

—*David McCasland*

Live the Christian life in the same way you began it—by trusting Christ.

✗

EVEN HER?

Read: Joshua 2:1-14

Was not even Rahab the prostitute considered righteous?
—JAMES 2:25

Imagine looking through your family tree and finding this description of your ancestor: "A prostitute, she harbored enemies of the government in her house. When she was confronted by the authorities, she lied about it."

What would you do about her? Hide her story from anyone inquiring about your family? Or spotlight and praise her in the legends of your family's story?

Meet Rahab. If what we read about her in Joshua 2 were all we knew, we might lump her in with all of the other renegades and bad examples in the Bible. But her story doesn't stop there. Matthew 1:5–6 reveals that she was King David's great-great grandmother—and that she was in the lineage of our Savior, Jesus. And there's more. Hebrews 11:31 names Rahab as a woman of faith who was saved from the fall of Jericho (see Joshua 6:17). And in James 2:25, her works of rescue were given as evidence of her righteous faith.

God's love is amazing that way. He can take people with a bad reputation, transform their lives, and turn them into examples of His love and forgiveness. If you think you're too bad to be forgiven or if you know someone else who feels that way, read about Rahab and rejoice. If God can turn her into a beacon of righteousness, there's hope for all of us.

—*Dave Branon*

Whether our sins are great or small, Jesus is able to forgive them all.

WE NEED HOPE

Read: Colossians 1:3-14

Blessed is the one who trusts in the LORD, whose confidence is in him.
—JEREMIAH 17:7

Adam and Eve didn't need hope because they didn't lack anything they needed. And they had every reason to think that life would go on as pleasantly as it started—with every good thing that God had given them to enjoy. But they put it all at risk for the one thing the serpent said that God had withheld: the knowledge of good and evil (Genesis 2:17; 3:5). So when the serpent came with his offer, Eve was quick to indulge, and Adam was quick to follow (3:6). They got what they wanted: knowledge. But they lost what they had: innocence. With the loss of innocence came the need for hope—hope that their guilt and shame could be removed and goodness restored.

This is why we love Christmas so much. No matter what time of year it is, we can recall the hope it brings to us. Children hope for the latest popular toy or game. Families hope that everyone can make it home for the holidays. But the hope that Christmas commemorates is much bigger than our holiday desires. Jesus, the "Desire of All Nations" (Haggai 2:7 NKJV), has come! He has "rescued us from the dominion of darkness," bought our redemption, and forgiven our sins (Colossians 1:13–14). He even made it possible for us to be wise about what is good and innocent about what is evil (Romans 16:19). Christ in us gives us the hope of glory.

Every day of the year, we can praise God for the hope of Christmas!

—*Julie Ackerman Link*

—

Hope for the Christian is a certainty—because its basis is Christ.

SEEING GOD
IN FAMILIAR PLACES

Read: Isaiah 6:1-6

The whole earth is full of his glory. —ISAIAH 6:3

Because of where I live, I'm treated to spectacular displays of the magnificent, creative glory of God. Recently, on a drive through the woods, I was struck with a breathtaking display of deep, rich reds and a variety of yellows that decorated the trees of autumn—all artfully arranged against the backdrop of a brilliant blue sky.

And later, as the temperatures plummet and winter blows in, I'll be reminded that no two snowflakes are ever the same as they pile on top of one another to create a rolling landscape of pristine white drifts. After that will come the miracle of spring, when that which seemed hopelessly dead bursts into life with buds and blossoms that will grace the meadows with a multiplicity of colors.

Wherever we look in the world around us, we see evidence that "the whole earth is full of [God's] glory" (Isaiah 6:3). What is amazing is that the creation that surrounds us is damaged by sin (see Romans 8:18–22), yet God has seen fit to grace our fallen landscape with these loving brushstrokes of His creative hand. It serves as a daily reminder that the beauty of His grace covers our sin and that His love for that which is fallen is always available to us.

—*Joe Stowell*

Never pass up an opportunity to enjoy nature's beauty—it's the handwriting of God.

NEW HOPE

Read: Romans 15:5-13

May the God of hope fill you with all joy and peace in believing, that you may abound in hope by the power of the Holy Spirit.
—ROMANS 15:13 NKJV

Grant Murphy of Seattle was the active type, a man who ran at full throttle. Idling and coasting were not in his nature. "One might even call him hyperactive," recalled a dear friend.

Then multiple sclerosis began to slow Grant down. First he needed crutches to get around. Then he was limited to sitting in a chair. Finally he was confined to a bed.

Near the end, he was hardly strong enough to talk. His friend recalls, however, that "he expressed only joy and thankfulness with a constant anticipation of being in the Lord's presence." Not long before he died, Grant whispered Romans 15:13 to a friend. He repeated the words "in believing," then added, "I can't do anything now."

It's when we can't do anything that God does everything. And herein lies a profound paradox of the Christian's experience. Faith is simultaneously an exercise of our will and the impartation of divine strength. And from that marvelous mixture spring joy and peace and an abundance of hope.

Are you in a totally helpless situation? Strength gone? All options exhausted? If you have trusted Jesus as your Savior, God will strengthen you to keep on believing. As you trust Him, He'll give you not only joy and peace, but also hope when all hope seems to be gone.

—*Dennis DeHaan*

No one is hopeless whose hope is in God.

SITUATION EXCELLENT

Read: Philippians 1:3-14

What has happened to me has actually served to advance the gospel.
—PHILIPPIANS 1:12

At the First Battle of the Marne during World War I, French lieutenant general Ferdinand Foch sent out this communiqué: "My center is giving way, my right is retreating. Situation excellent. I am attacking." His willingness to see hope in a tough situation eventually led to victory for his troops.

Sometimes in life's battles we can feel as if we are losing on every front. Family discord, business setbacks, financial woes, or a decline in health can put a pessimistic spin on the way we look at life. But the believer in Christ can always find a way to conclude: "Situation excellent."

Look at Paul. When he was thrown in prison for preaching the gospel, he had an unusually upbeat attitude. To the church at Philippi he wrote, "I want you to know, brothers and sisters, that what has happened to me has actually served to advance the gospel" (Philippians 1:12).

Paul saw his prison situation as a new platform from which to evangelize the Roman palace guard. In addition, other Christians became emboldened by his situation to preach the gospel fearlessly (vv. 13–14).

God can use our trials to "work for the good" in our lives in spite of the pain they bring (Romans 8:28). That's just one more way He can be honored.

—*Dennis Fisher*

Trials can be God's road to triumph.

𝄪

HEARTBREAK AND HOPE

Read: Lamentations 3:1-6; 16-25

The LORD is good to those whose hope is in him, to the one who seeks him.
—LAMENTATIONS 3:25

When American country singer George Jones died at the age of 81, his fans remembered his remarkable voice and his hard life and personal struggles. While many of his songs reflected his own despair and longing, it was the way he sang them that touched people deeply. *Chicago Tribune* music critic Greg Kot said Jones's voice was "made for conveying heartbreak."

The book of Lamentations records Jeremiah's anguish over the nation of Judah's stubborn refusal to follow God. Often called "the weeping prophet," he witnessed the destruction of Jerusalem and saw his people carried into captivity. He wandered the streets of the city, overwhelmed by grief (Lamentations 1:1–5).

Yet, in Jeremiah's darkest hour, he said, "This I call to mind, and therefore I have hope. Because of the LORD's great love we are not consumed, for his compassions never fail. They are new every morning; great is your faithfulness" (3:21–23).

Whether we suffer for our own choices or from those of others, despair may threaten to overwhelm us. When all seems lost, we can cling to the Lord's faithfulness. "'The LORD is my portion; therefore I will wait for him'" (v. 24).

—*David McCasland*

The anchor of God's faithfulness holds firm in the strongest storms.

LONGING FOR HOME

Read: Hebrews 11:8–16

They were longing for a better country—a heavenly one.
—HEBREWS 11:16

My wife walked into the room and found me poking my head inside the cabinet of our grandfather clock. "What are you doing?" she asked. "This clock smells just like my parents' house," I answered sheepishly, closing the door. "I guess you could say I was going home for a moment."

The sense of smell can evoke powerful memories. We had moved the clock across the country from my parents' house nearly twenty years ago, but the aroma of the wood inside the cabinet still takes me back to my childhood.

The writer of Hebrews tells of others who were longing for home in a different way. Instead of looking backward, they were looking ahead with faith to their home in heaven. Even though what they hoped for seemed a long way off, they trusted that God was faithful to keep His promise to bring them to a place where they would be with Him forever (Hebrews 11:13–16).

Philippians 3:20 reminds us that "our citizenship is in heaven," and we are to "eagerly await a Savior from there, the Lord Jesus Christ." Looking forward to seeing Jesus and receiving everything God has promised us through Him helps us keep our focus. The past or the present can never compare with what's ahead of us!

—*James Banks*

The best home of all is our home in heaven.

A REASON FOR HOPE

Read: Lamentations 3:19-33

His compassions never fail. They are new every morning; great is your faithfulness. —LAMENTATIONS 3:22–23

It's one of the saddest stories of the Bible, yet it inspired one of the most hopeful hymns of the twentieth century.

The prophet Jeremiah witnessed unimaginable horrors when the Babylonians invaded Jerusalem in 586 BC. Solomon's temple was reduced to ruins, and with it went not only the center of worship but also the heart of the community. The people were left with no food, no rest, no peace, no leader. But in the midst of suffering and grief, one of their prophets found a reason for hope. "Because of the LORD's great love we are not consumed," wrote Jeremiah, "for his compassions never fail. They are new every morning; great is your faithfulness" (Lamentations 3:22–23).

Jeremiah's hope came from his personal experience of the Lord's faithfulness and from his knowledge of God's promises in the past. Without these, he would have been unable to comfort his people.

This hope of Lamentations 3 is echoed in a hymn by Thomas Chisholm (1866–1960). Although suffering sickness and setbacks throughout his life, he wrote "Great Is Thy Faithfulness." This song reminds us that even in times of great fear, tragic loss, and intense suffering we can find comfort and confidence as we trust in God's great faithfulness.

—*Julie Ackerman Link*

The best reason for hope is God's faithfulness.

IT'S IN THE WORD

Read: Psalm 119:25-32

I run the path of your commands, for you have broadened my understanding. —PSALM 119:32

As optimistic as I am (I can find a bright side to just about everything), I also know that life can be a dark and lonely place.

I've talked to teenagers who have a parent whose anger makes just going home after school a dreaded trip.

I've known people who can't escape the curtain of depression.

I've spent considerable time with others who, like my wife and me, are enduring life with the sudden death of a child.

I've seen what relentless poverty can do to people all over the world.

Despite knowing that these scenarios exist, I don't despair. I know that hope is available in Jesus, that guidance comes through the Spirit, and that knowledge and power are found in God's Word.

The words of Psalm 119 give us encouragement. When our soul is "laid low in the dust," we can be revived according to God's Word (v. 25). When our soul is full of sorrow, we can be strengthened by the same source (v. 28). When we are threatened by deceit, we can follow God's laws (vv. 29–30). We can be given new understanding through God's commands (v. 32).

Are life's demands overwhelming you? If so, you can find hope, guidance, and knowledge to help. It's in God's Word.

—*Dave Branon*

A well-read Bible makes a well-fed soul.

WORDS FOR THE WEARY

Read: Isaiah 50:4-10

The Sovereign LORD has given me a well-instructed tongue, to know the word that sustains the weary. —ISAIAH 50:4

A few days after his father died, thirty-year-old C. S. Lewis received a letter from a woman who had cared for his mother during her illness and death more than two decades earlier. The woman offered her sympathy for his loss and wondered if he remembered her. "My dear Nurse Davison," Lewis replied. "Remember you? I should think I do."

Lewis recalled how much her presence in their home had meant to him as well as to his brother and father during a difficult time. He thanked her for her words of sympathy and said, "It is *really* comforting to be taken back to those old days. The time during which you were with my mother seemed very long to a child and you became part of home."

When we struggle in the circumstances of life, an encouraging word from others can lift our spirits and direct our eyes to the Lord. The Old Testament prophet Isaiah wrote, "The Sovereign LORD has given me a well-instructed tongue, to know the word that sustains the weary" (50:4). And when we look to the Lord, He offers words of hope and light in the darkness.

—*David McCasland*

Kind words can lift a heavy heart.

✕

THE CROSS AND THE CROWN

Read: John 19:21–30

Jesus said . . . , "I am the resurrection and the life. The one who believes in me will live, even though they die." —JOHN 11:25

Westminster Abbey in London has a rich historical background. In the tenth century, Benedictine monks began a tradition of daily worship there that still continues today. The Abbey is also the burial place of many famous people, and every English monarch since AD 1066 has been crowned at the Abbey. In fact, seventeen of those monarchs are also buried there—their rule ending where it began.

No matter how grandiose their burial, world rulers rise and fall; they live and die. But another king, Jesus, though once dead, is no longer buried. In His first coming, Jesus was crowned with thorns and crucified as the "king of the Jews" (John 19:3, 19). Because Jesus rose from the dead in victory, we who are believers in Christ have hope beyond the grave and the assurance that we will live with Him forever. Jesus said, "I am the resurrection and the life. The one who believes in me will live, even though they die; and whoever lives by believing in me will never die" (11:25–26).

We serve a risen King! May we gladly yield to His rule in our lives now as we look forward to the day when the "Lord God Almighty" will reign for all eternity (Revelation 19:6).

—*Bill Crowder*

Jesus's resurrection spelled the death of death.

THE BLESSED HOPE

Read: 2 Peter 3:10-18

We wait for the blessed hope—the appearing of the glory
of our great God and Savior, Jesus Christ. —TITUS 2:13

So many predictions of the end of the world have come and gone. Those predictions are unsettling and often fill people with fear. Yet the Bible does refer to a time called "the day of the Lord" when He will return (1 Thessalonians 5:2). It will happen, but only God knows when.

It's a day that Jesus's followers can look forward to. In light of that time to come, the apostle Peter tells us how the believer can live with a joyful purpose (2 Peter 3:10–18). We can look upward by living Christ-honoring lives (v. 11). We can look inward by making every effort to be found at peace with God (v. 14). And we can look outward by being on guard so we aren't carried away by the wrong influence of others (v. 17).

How do we do this? By "grow[ing] in the grace and knowledge of our Lord and Savior Jesus Christ" (v. 18). When we grow in character through His written Word, we begin to relate more closely to Jesus, the Living Word. The Holy Spirit takes God's Word and guides us in the way to live.

The day of the Lord shouldn't be a fearful day for Jesus's followers. Our King will return to make all things right and to rule forever. We wait for that time with great anticipation. It is our "blessed hope" (Titus 2:13).

—*C. P. Hia*

One day Jesus will return to rule and reign!

COMING SOON

Read: Revelation 22:7-21

"Yes, I am coming soon." —REVELATION 22:20

A "COMING SOON!" announcement often precedes future events in entertainment and sports, or the launch of the latest technology. The goal is to create anticipation and excitement for what is going to happen, even though it may be months away.

While reading the book of Revelation, I was impressed with the "coming soon" sense of immediacy permeating the entire book. Rather than saying, "Someday, in the far distant future, Jesus Christ is going to return to earth," the text is filled with phrases like "what must soon take place" (1:1) and "the time is near" (v. 3). Three times in the final chapter, the Lord says, "I am coming soon" (Revelation 22:7, 12, 20). Other versions translate this phrase as "I am coming quickly" (NKJV) and "I'm on my way!" (MSG, paraphrase).

How can this be—since two thousand years have elapsed since these words were written? "Soon" doesn't seem appropriate for our experience of time.

Rather than focusing on a date for His return, the Lord is urging us to set our hearts on His promise that will be fulfilled. We are called to live for Him in this present age as we "wait for the blessed hope—the appearing of the glory of our great God and Savior Jesus Christ" (Titus 2:13).

—David McCasland

———

Live as if Christ is coming back today.

FROM BLEAK TO BEAUTIFUL

Read: Job 42:10-17

The LORD blessed the latter part of Job's life more than the former part.
—JOB 42:12

Spring is the time of year when God reminds us that things are not always as they seem. Over the course of a few short weeks, what appears hopelessly dead comes to life. Bleak woodlands are transformed into colorful landscapes. Trees whose naked arms reached to heaven all winter, as if pleading to be clothed, suddenly are adorned with lacy green gowns. Flowers that faded and fell to the ground in surrender to the cold rise slowly from the earth in defiance of death.

In Scripture, we read about some apparently hopeless situations. One example is that of a wealthy man named Job whom God described as having integrity (Job 2:3). Disaster struck and Job lost everything important to him. In misery, he said, "My days . . . come to an end without hope" (7:6). What appeared to Job and his friends as evidence that God had turned against him was just the opposite. God was so confident of Job's integrity that He trusted him in this battle with Satan. Later, Job's hope and life were renewed.

The faithful arrival of spring every year comforts me when I'm in a situation that seems hopeless. With God, there is no such thing. No matter how bleak the landscape of life may look, God can transform it into a glorious garden of color and fragrance.

—*Julie Ackerman Link*

———

With God, there is hope even in the most hopeless situation.

HOPE IN GOD

Read: Psalm 42

Why, my soul, are you downcast? . . . Put your hope in God,
for I will yet praise him, my Savior and my God. —PSALM 42:5

Looking at the western shores of Sri Lanka, I found it hard to imagine that a tsunami had struck just a few months earlier. The sea was calm and beautiful, couples were walking in the bright sunshine, and people were going about their business—all giving the scene an ordinary feeling I wasn't prepared for. The impact of the disaster was still there, but it had gone underground into the hearts and minds of the survivors. The trauma itself would not be easily forgotten.

It was catastrophic grief that prompted the psalmist to cry out in anguish: "My tears have been my food day and night, while people say to me all day long, 'Where is your God?'" (Psalm 42:3). The struggle of his heart had likewise been turned inward. While the rest of the world went on with business as usual, he carried in his heart the need for deep and complete healing.

Only as we submit our brokenness to the good and great Shepherd of our hearts can we find the peace that allows us to respond to life: "Why, my soul, are you downcast? . . . Put your hope in God, for I will yet praise him, my Savior and my God" (v. 5).

Hope in God—it's the only solution for the deep traumas of the heart.

—*Bill Crowder*

A world without Christ would be
a world without hope.

✗

ALL SAFE! ALL WELL!

Read: Hebrews 11:8-16

Now faith is confidence in what we hope for and assurance about what we do not see. —HEBREWS 11:1

In January 1915, the ship *Endurance* was trapped and crushed in the ice off the coast of Antarctica. The group of polar explorers, led by Ernest Shackleton, survived and managed to reach Elephant Island in three small lifeboats. Trapped on this uninhabited island, far from normal shipping lanes, they had one hope. On April 24, 1916, twenty-two men watched as Shackleton and five comrades set out in a tiny lifeboat for South Georgia, an island more than eight hundred miles away. The odds seemed impossible, and if they failed, they would all certainly die. What joy, then, when more than *four months* later a boat appeared on the horizon with Shackleton on its bow shouting to his men on Elephant Island, "Are you all well?" And the call came back, "All safe! All well!"

What held those men together and kept them alive over those months? Faith and hope placed in one man. They believed that Shackleton would find a way to save them.

This human example of faith and hope echoes the faith of the heroes listed in Hebrews 11. Their faith in the "substance of things hoped for, the evidence of things not seen" kept them going through great difficulties and trials (Hebrews 11:1 NKJV).

As we look out upon the horizon of our own problems, may we not despair. May we have hope through the certainty of our faith in the One Man—Jesus, our God and Savior.

—*Randy Kilgore*

The hope of Jesus shines brightly even on our darkest day.

HOPE WHEN THE JOURNEY GETS TOUGH

Read: 2 Corinthians 1:6–11

We should not trust in ourselves but in God who raises the dead.
—2 CORINTHIANS 1:9 NKJV

In August 2009, Blair and Ronna Martin lost their energetic nine-year-old son Matti when he was dragged to his death by a family cow. I had a chance to meet this Kenai, Alaska, family and share in their grief. And I know how tough this tragedy has been for them.

I also know that they are seeking God's care and comfort for their pain. An observation made by Matti's mom is valuable for anyone walking through one of life's valleys. During one of her down times, Ronna was reading 2 Corinthians 1:9, which says, "We should not trust in ourselves but in God who raises the dead." She felt as if Jesus were telling her, "Ronna, I know the journey has been too much for you, and you are bone-weary. Do not be ashamed of your exhaustion. Instead, see it as an opportunity for Me to take charge of your life."

When the journey gets too tough to navigate, 2 Corinthians 1:9 is a reminder to us that we don't travel alone. We have the help of the One who showed us His power in the resurrection and who will demonstrate His power again when He raises believing loved ones of all generations to eternal life. "My strength and my hope have to be in Christ alone," Ronna said. That's a truth we all need as we travel the journey God has for us.

—*Dave Branon*

The storms of life remind us to take shelter in the loving arms of our Savior.

WAITING

Read: Psalm 130

Be joyful in hope, patient in affliction, faithful in prayer.
—ROMANS 12:12

Day after day for years Harry shared with the Lord his concern for his son-in-law John, who had turned away from God. But then Harry died. A few months later, John turned back to God. When his mother-in-law Marsha told him that Harry had been praying for him every day, John replied, "I waited too long." But Marsha joyfully shared: "The Lord is still answering the prayers Harry prayed during his earthly life."

Harry's story is an encouragement to us who pray and wait. He continued "faithful in prayer" and waited patiently (Romans 12:12).

The author of Psalm 130 experienced waiting in prayer. He said, "I wait for the LORD, my whole being waits" (v. 5). He found hope in God because he knew that "with the LORD is unfailing love and with him is full redemption" (v. 7).

Author Samuel Enyia wrote about God's timing: "God does not depend on our time. Our time is chronological and linear but God . . . is timeless. He will act at the fullness of His time. Our prayer . . . may not necessarily rush God into action, but . . . places us before Him in fellowship."

What a privilege we have to fellowship with God in prayer and to wait for the answer in the fullness of His time.

—*Anne Cetas*

God may delay our request, but He will never disappoint our trust.

CAN'T DIE BUT ONCE

Read: Matthew 6:26-32

Do not be afraid of those who kill the body but cannot kill the soul.
—MATTHEW 10:28

Born into slavery and badly treated as a young girl, Harriet Tubman (c. 1822–1913) found a shining ray of hope in the Bible stories her mother told. The account of Israel's escape from slavery under Pharaoh showed her a God who desired freedom for His people.

Harriet found freedom when she slipped over the Maryland state line and out of slavery. She couldn't remain content, however, knowing so many were still trapped in captivity. So she led more than a dozen rescue missions to free those still in slavery, dismissing the personal danger. "I can't die but once," she said.

Harriet knew the truth of the statement: "Do not be afraid of those who kill the body but cannot kill the soul" (Matthew 10:28). Jesus spoke those words as He sent His disciples on their first mission. He knew they would face danger, and not everyone would receive them warmly. So why expose the disciples to the risk? The answer is found in the previous chapter. "When he saw the crowds, [Jesus] had compassion on them, because they were harassed and helpless, like sheep without a shepherd" (9:36).

When Harriet Tubman couldn't forget those still trapped in slavery, she showed us a picture of Christ, who did not forget us when we were trapped in our sins. Her courageous example inspires us to remember those who remain without hope in the world.

—*Tim Gustafson*

True freedom is found in knowing and serving Christ.

NOT WITHOUT HOPE

Read: Exodus 6:1-13

I will free you from being slaves to them, and I will redeem you
with an outstretched arm and with mighty acts of judgment.
—EXODUS 6:6

"Sixteen Tons," written by Merle Travis and recorded by Tennessee Ernie Ford, became one of America's most popular songs in the mid-1950s. People seemed to identify with this coal miner's lament about feeling trapped and unable to change his situation no matter how hard he worked. Coal miners often lived in company-owned houses and were paid in "scrip"—coupons valid only at the company-owned store. Even if summoned to heaven, the miner said, he couldn't go because he owed his soul to the company store.

That sense of hopeless resignation may help us understand the feelings of the Hebrew people during their 400 years of bondage in Egypt. When Moses told them of God's promise to release them from slavery, they didn't listen to him "because of their discouragement" (Exodus 6:9). They were so far down they couldn't look up.

But God did something for them that they could not do for themselves. The Lord's miraculous deliverance of His people foreshadowed His powerful intervention on our behalf through His Son Jesus Christ. It was when "we were powerless to help ourselves that Christ died for sinful men" (Romans 5:6 PHILLIPS).

When life is at its lowest ebb, trust God. Because of His wonderful grace, we are never without hope.

—*David McCasland*

When you feel hopeless,
look to the God of hope.

〤

FROM MOURNING TO DANCING

Read: Isaiah 61:1-4

He has sent me . . . to bestow on [those who grieve] a crown of beauty
instead of ashes, the oil of joy instead of mourning.
—ISAIAH 61:1, 3

"We're cutting your job." A decade ago those words sent me reeling when the company I worked for eliminated my position. At the time, I felt shattered, partly because my identity was so intertwined with my role as editor. Recently I felt a similar sadness when I heard that my freelance job was ending. But this time I didn't feel rocked at my foundation, because over the years I have seen God's faithfulness and how He can turn my mourning to joy.

Though we live in a fallen world where we experience pain and disappointment, the Lord can move us from despair to rejoicing, as we see in Isaiah's prophecy about the coming of Jesus (Isaiah 61:1–3). The Lord gives us hope when we feel hopeless; He helps us to forgive when we think we can't; He teaches us that our identity is in Him and not in what we do. He gives us courage to face an unknown future. When we wear the rags of "ashes," He gently gives us a coat of praise.

When we face loss, we shouldn't run from the sadness, but neither do we want to become bitter or hardened. When we think about God's faithfulness over the years, we know that He's willing and able to turn our grief to dancing once again—to give us sufficient grace in this life and full joy in heaven.

—*Amy Boucher Pye*

———

God can bring times of growth out of our times of heartache.

THE BOOK OF HOPE

Read: Romans 5:1-11

Hope does not disappoint. —ROMANS 5:5 NKJV

Writing in *Texas Co-Op Power* magazine, Donna Chapman described the excitement generated on her family's farm in the 1940s by the arrival of the Montgomery Ward catalog. Often called "the wish book," its pages were filled with images of items ranging from clothing and cookstoves to furniture and tools. The catalog's warm, friendly tone seemed to invite people to picture themselves as they lived, worked, and dressed at the time, and as they hoped to become.

The Bible is not a spiritual mail-order catalog, but in its pages we vividly see ourselves both as we are today and as we hope to be. The Bible certainly is God's book of hope.

In Romans 5, Paul said that "we boast in the hope of the glory of God" (v. 2), "glory in our sufferings" (v. 3), and "boast in God through our Lord Jesus Christ" (v. 11). Even our present difficulties are an essential part of the process of becoming the people we know God wants us to be.

The Bible is far more than a book of wishful thinking; it is a book of well-founded confidence in God's purpose and plan for us as believers. Whatever we are like today, we know that in Christ we have a living hope, and it will not end in disappointment.

—*David McCasland*

God's living Word is the only hope for a dying world.

AN AMAZING LOVE

Read: Malachi 1:1-10; 4:5-6

"I have loved you," says the LORD. —MALACHI 1:2

The final major historic acts of the Old Testament are described in Ezra and Nehemiah as God allowed the people of Israel to return from exile and resettle in Jerusalem. The City of David was repopulated with Hebrew families, a new temple was built, and the wall was repaired.

And that brings us to Malachi. This prophet, who was most likely a contemporary of Nehemiah, brings the written portion of the Old Testament to a close. Notice the first thing he said to the people of Israel: "'I have loved you,' says the LORD." And look at their response: "How have you loved us?" (1:2).

Amazing, isn't it? Their history had proven God's faithfulness, yet after hundreds of years in which God continually provided for His chosen people in both miraculous and mundane ways, they wondered how He had shown His love. As the book continues, Malachi reminds the people of their unfaithfulness (see vv. 6–8). They had a long historical pattern of God's provision for them, followed by their disobedience, followed by God's discipline.

It would be time, soon, for a new way. The prophet hints at it in Malachi 4:5–6. The Messiah would be coming. There was hope ahead for a Savior who would show us His love and pay the penalty once and for all for our sin.

That Messiah indeed has come! Malachi's hope is now a reality in Jesus.

—*Dave Branon*

———

Those who put their trust in Jesus will have eternal life.

LET US . . .

Read: Hebrews 10:19-25

*Let us consider how we may spur one another on toward love
and good deeds.* —HEBREWS 10:24

While standing in line for a popular attraction at Disneyland, I noticed that most people were talking and smiling instead of complaining about the long wait. It made me ponder what made waiting in that line an enjoyable experience. The key seemed to be that very few people were there by themselves. Instead, friends, families, groups, and couples were sharing the experience, which was far different than standing in line alone.

The Christian life is meant to be lived in company with others, not alone. In Hebrews 10:19–25 the writer urges us to live in community with other followers of Jesus. "Let us draw near to God with a sincere heart and with the full assurance that faith brings . . . . Let us hold unswervingly to the hope we profess, for he who promised is faithful. And let us consider how we may spur one another on toward love and good deeds, not giving up meeting together" (vv. 22–25). In community we reassure and reinforce each other by "encouraging one another" (v. 25).

Even our most difficult days can become a meaningful part of our journey of faith when others share them with us. Don't face life alone. Let us travel together.

—*David McCasland*

Life in Christ is meant to be a shared experience.

RIPPLES OF HOPE

Read: 1 Peter 1:3-9

In his great mercy he has given us new birth into a living hope
through the resurrection of Jesus Christ from the dead.
—1 PETER 1:3

In 1966, US Senator Robert Kennedy made an influential visit to South Africa. There he offered words of hope to opponents of apartheid in his famous "Ripple of Hope" speech at the University of Cape Town. In his speech, he declared, "Each time a man stands up for an ideal, or acts to improve the lot of others, or strikes out against injustice, he sends forth a tiny ripple of hope, and crossing each other from a million different centers of energy and daring, those ripples build a current which can sweep down the mightiest walls of oppression and resistance."

At times in this world, hope seems scarce. Yet there is an ultimate hope readily available for the follower of Christ. Peter wrote, "Praise be to the God and Father of our Lord Jesus Christ! In his great mercy he has given us new birth into a living hope through the resurrection of Jesus Christ from the dead" (1 Peter 1:3).

Through the certainty of Christ's resurrection, the child of God has a hope that is more than a ripple. It is an overwhelming current of confidence in the faithfulness of the One who conquered death for us. Jesus, in His victory over death—our greatest enemy—can infuse hope into the most hopeless of situations.

—*Bill Crowder*

In Christ, the hopeless find hope.

𝕏

ALWAYS

Read: 1 Thessalonians 4:13-18

We will be with the Lord forever. Therefore encourage one another with these words. —1 THESSALONIANS 4:17–18

I love the words *always* and *never*. They hold so much hope! I would like to think that I could *always* be happy and that life would *never* fail me. But reality says that I won't always be happy and that the things I hope would never happen just might. So, as good as these words sound, they struggle to live up to their potential—unless you are thinking about the promise of Jesus's presence.

To a group of troubled disciples who feared facing life on their own Jesus said, "I am with you always" (Matthew 28:20). The writer to the Hebrews reminds us that Jesus said, "'Never will I leave you; never will I forsake you.' So we may with confidence say: 'The Lord is my helper; I will not be afraid'" (Hebrews 13:5–6). And the apostle Paul assures believers that after death, "We will be with the Lord forever" (1 Thessalonians 4:17). How encouraging!

No matter how scary our journey may feel today or how hopeless our future may look, the assurance of His never-failing presence can provide us with the courage and comfort to make it through. And best of all, when this short life is over, we will always be with Him. No wonder Paul tells us to "encourage one another with these words" (v. 18).

—*Joe Stowell*

———

Confidence in God's presence is our comfort.

HE WALKED IN OUR SHOES

Read: Hebrews 2:10-18

Because he himself suffered when he was tempted, he is able to help those who are being tempted. —HEBREWS 2:18

To help his staff of young architects understand the needs of those for whom they design housing, David Dillard sends them on "sleepovers." They put on pajamas and spend twenty-four hours in a senior living center in the same conditions as people in their eighties and nineties. They wear earplugs to simulate hearing loss, tape their fingers together to limit manual dexterity, and exchange eyeglasses to replicate vision problems. Dillard says, "The biggest benefit is [that] when I send twenty-seven-year-olds out, they come back with a heart ten times as big. They meet people and understand their plights" (Rodney Brooks, *USA Today*).

Jesus lived on this earth for thirty-three years and shared in our humanity. He was made like us, "fully human in every way" (Hebrews 2:17), so He knows what it's like to live in a human body on this earth. He understands the struggles we face and comes alongside with understanding and encouragement.

"Because [Jesus] himself suffered when he was tempted, he is able to help those who are being tempted" (v. 18). The Lord could have avoided the cross. Instead, He obeyed His Father. Through His death, He broke the power of Satan and freed us from our fear of death (vv. 14–15).

In every temptation, Jesus walks beside us to give us courage, strength, and hope along the way.

—*David McCasland*

Jesus understands.

HOPE BEYOND HOPE

Read: Jeremiah 17:1-8

Blessed is the one who trusts in the LORD, whose confidence is in him.
—JEREMIAH 17:7

The English poet Alexander Pope (1688–1744) wrote, "Hope springs eternal in the human breast: Man never is, but always to be blest." But where does man turn when hope dries up?

The director of a medical clinic told the story of a terminally ill young man who came in for his usual treatment. A new doctor who was on duty said to him casually and cruelly, "You know, don't you, that you won't live out the year?"

As the young man left, he stopped by the director's desk and wept. "That man took away my hope," he blurted out.

"I guess he did," replied the director. "Maybe it's time to find a new one."

Commenting on this incident, theologian Lewis Smedes (1921–2002) wrote, "Is there a hope when hope is taken away? Is there hope when the situation is hopeless? That question leads us to Christian hope, for in the Bible, hope is no longer a passion for the possible. It becomes a passion for the promise."

When our expectation is rooted in God and in His Son Jesus Christ as our Savior from sin and death, the blessing that Alexander Pope says we are always looking for becomes a present reality. Because God is the God of hope (Romans 15:13), He alone keeps hope flowing when its springs dry up in the human breast.

—*Dennis DeHaan*

The secret of coping is hoping in God.

SUCH A HOPE

Read: Romans 8:18-27

We have this hope as an anchor for the soul, firm and secure.
It enters the inner sanctuary behind the curtain.
—HEBREWS 6:19

Two women. One a former coworker I had known for twenty years. The other, the wife of a former student from my days as a schoolteacher. Both dedicated moms of two young children. Both missionaries. Both incredibly in love with Jesus Christ.

Then suddenly, within the space of a month—both were dead. The first, Sharon Fasick, died in a car accident, attracting little attention though deeply affecting family and friends. The second, Roni Bowers, died with her daughter Charity when their plane was shot down over the jungles of Peru—a situation that thrust her story into the international spotlight.

Their deaths filled many people with inexpressible sorrow. But there was something else—hope. Both women's husbands had the confident expectation that they would see their wives again in heaven. What happened after they died demonstrates that the Christian faith works. Both men, Jeff Fasick and Jim Bowers, have spoken about the peace God has given them. They have testified that this kind of hope has allowed them to continue on in the midst of the unspeakable pain.

Paul said that our present sufferings "are not worth comparing with the glory that will be revealed in us" (Romans 8:18). Such a hope comes only from Christ.

—*Dave Branon*

The hope of heaven is God's solution for sorrow.

RESCUE FROM DESPAIR

Read: Judges 13:1-7

He will take the lead in delivering Israel from the hands of the Philistines.
—JUDGES 13:5

When a powerful typhoon swept through the city of Tacloban, Philippines, in 2013, an estimated 10,000 people died, and many who survived found themselves homeless and jobless. Necessities became scarce. Three months later, while the town was still struggling to dig itself out from the destruction, a baby was born on a roadside near Tacloban amid torrents of rain and strong wind. Although the weather brought back painful memories, residents worked together to find a midwife and transport the mother and newborn to a clinic. The baby survived, thrived, and became a symbol of hope during a time of despair.

Forty years of Philistine oppression marked a grim period in Israel's national history. During this time, an angel informed an Israelite woman that she would give birth to a special son (Judges 13:3). According to the angel, the baby would be a Nazirite—a man set apart to God—and would "begin to deliver Israel out of the hand of the Philistines" (v. 5). The infant, Samson, was a gift of hope born in a troubled time.

Trouble is unavoidable, yet Jesus has the power to rescue us from despair. Christ was born "to shine on those sitting in darkness and in the shadow of death, to guide our feet into the path of peace" (Luke 1:76–79).

—*Jennifer Benson Schuldt*

Jesus is the hope that calms life's storms.

𝕏

GOOD NEWS

Read: Nahum 1:7-15

Look, there on the mountains, the feet of one who brings good news, who proclaims peace! —NAHUM 1:15

World news bombards us from the Internet, television, radio, and mobile devices. The majority seems to describe what's wrong—crime, terrorism, war, and economic problems. Yet there are times when good news invades the darkest hours of sadness and despair—stories of unselfish acts, a medical breakthrough, or steps toward peace in war-scarred places.

The words of two men recorded in the Old Testament of the Bible brought great hope to people weary of conflict.

While describing God's coming judgment on a ruthless and powerful nation, Nahum said, "Look, there on the mountains, the feet of one who brings good news, who proclaims peace!" (Nahum 1:15). That news brought hope to all those oppressed by cruelty.

A similar phrase occurs in the book of Isaiah: "How beautiful on the mountains are the feet of those who bring good news, who proclaim peace, who bring good tidings, who proclaim salvation" (Isaiah 52:7).

Nahum and Isaiah's prophetic words of hope found their ultimate fulfillment at the first Christmas when the angel told the shepherds, "Do not be afraid. I bring you good news that will cause great joy for all the people. Today in the town of David a Savior has been born to you; he is the Messiah, the Lord" (Luke 2:10–11).

The most important headline in our lives every day is the very best news ever spoken—Christ the Savior is born!

—*David McCasland*

The birth of Jesus is the best news the world has ever received!

OUR DAILY BREAD WRITERS

JAMES BANKS

Pastor of Peace Church in Durham, North Carolina, Dr. James Banks has written several books for Discovery House, including *Praying Together* and *Prayers for Prodigals.*

DAVE BRANON

An editor with Discovery House, Dave has been involved with *Our Daily Bread* since the 1980s. He has written several books, including *Beyond the Valley* and *Stand Firm*, both DH publications.

ANNE CETAS

After becoming a Christian in her late teens, Anne was introduced to *Our Daily Bread* right away and began reading it. Now she reads it for a living as senior content editor of *Our Daily Bread.*

POH FANG CHIA

Like Anne Cetas, Poh Fang trusted Jesus Christ as Savior as a teenager. She is an editor and a part of the Chinese editorial review committee serving in the Our Daily Bread Ministries Singapore office.

BILL CROWDER

A former pastor who is now vice president of content teaching for Our Daily Bread Ministries, Bill travels extensively as a Bible conference teacher, sharing God's truths with fellow believers in Malaysia and Singapore and other places where ODB Ministries has international offices. His Discovery House books include *Windows on Easter* and *Let's Talk.*

DENNIS DEHAAN (1932-2014)

When Henry Bosch retired, Dennis became the second managing editor of *Our Daily Bread*. A former pastor, he loved preaching and teaching the Word of God. Dennis went to be with the Lord in 2014.

RICHARD DEHAAN (1923-2002)

Son of the founder of Our Daily Bread Ministries, Dr. M. R. DeHaan, Richard was responsible for the ministry's entrance into television. Under his leadership, *Day of Discovery* television made its debut in 1968.

DAVID EGNER

A retired Our Daily Bread Ministries editor and longtime *Our Daily Bread* writer, David was also a college professor during his working career. In fact, he was a writing instructor for both Anne Cetas and Julie Ackerman Link at Cornerstone University.

DENNIS FISHER

As a senior research editor at Our Daily Bread Ministries, Dennis uses his theological training to guarantee biblical accuracy. He is also an expert in C. S. Lewis studies.

VERNON GROUNDS (1914-2010)

A longtime college president (Denver Seminary) and board member for Our Daily Bread Ministries, Vernon's life story was told in the Discovery House book *Transformed by Love*. Dr. Grounds died in 2010 at the age of 96.

TIM GUSTAFSON

Tim writes for *Our Daily Bread* and *Our Daily Journey* and serves as an editor for Discovery Series. As the son of missionaries to Ghana, Tim has an unusual perspective on life in the West. He and his wife, Leisa, are the parents of one daughter and seven sons.

C. P. HIA

A resident of Singapore, C. P. has been a men's Bible study leader for the past twenty years, and he also volunteers his services in the Our Daily Bread office in his homeland—the only island city-state in the world. He first wrote for *Our Daily Bread* in 2008.

CINDY HESS KASPER

An editor for the Our Daily Bread Ministries publication *Our Daily Journey*, Cindy began writing for *Our Daily Bread* in 2006. She and her husband, Tom, have three children and seven grandchildren.

RANDY KILGORE

Randy spent most of his twenty-plus years in business as a senior human resource manager before returning to seminary. Since finishing his Masters in Divinity in 2000, he has served as a writer and workplace chaplain. A collection of his devotionals appears in the Discovery House book *Made to Matter: Devotions for Working Christians*. Randy and his wife, Cheryl, and their two children live in Massachusetts.

JULIE ACKERMAN LINK (1950–2015)

A book editor by profession, Julie began writing for *Our Daily Bread* in 2000. Her books *Above All, Love* and *A Heart for God* are available through Discovery House. Julie lost her long battle with cancer in April 2015.

DAVID MCCASLAND

Living in Colorado, David enjoys the beauty of God's grandeur as displayed in the Rocky Mountains. An accomplished biographer, David has written several books, including the award-winning *Oswald Chambers: Abandoned to God* and *Eric Liddell: Pure Gold.*

AMY BOUCHER PYE

Amy is a writer, editor, and speaker. The author of *Finding Myself in Britain: Our Search for Faith, Home, and True Identity*, she runs the Woman Alive book club in the UK and enjoys life with her family in their English vicarage.

HADDON ROBINSON

Haddon, a renowned expert on preaching, served many years as a seminary professor. He wrote numerous books and hundreds of magazine articles. For a number of years he was a panelist on Our Daily Bread Ministries' radio program *Discover the Word.*

DAVID ROPER

David Roper lives in Idaho, where he takes advantage of the natural beauty of his state. He has been writing for *Our Daily Bread* since 2000, and he has published several successful books with Discovery House, including *Out of the Ordinary* and *Teach Us to Number Our Days.*

JENNIFER BENSON SCHULDT

Chicagoan Jennifer Schuldt writes from the perspective of a mom of a growing family. She has written for *Our Daily Bread* since 2010, and she also pens articles for another Our Daily Bread Ministries publication: *Our Daily Journey*.

JOE STOWELL

As president of Cornerstone University, Joe stays connected to today's young adults in a leadership role. A popular speaker and a former pastor, Joe has written a number of books over the years, including *Strength for the Journey* and *Jesus Nation*.

HERB VANDER LUGT (1920–2006)

For many years, Herb was senior research editor at Our Daily Bread Ministries, responsible for checking the biblical accuracy of the booklets published by ODB Ministries. A World War II veteran, Herb spent several years as a pastor before his ODB tenure began. Herb went to be with his Lord and Savior in 2006.

MARVIN WILLIAMS

Marvin's first foray into Our Daily Bread Ministries came as a writer for *Our Daily Journey*. In 2007, he penned his first *Our Daily Bread* article. Marvin is senior teaching pastor at a church in Lansing, Michigan. His book *Radical Generosity* is a Discovery House publication.

JOANIE YODER (1934–2004)

For ten years, until her death in 2004, Joanie wrote for *Our Daily Bread*. In addition, she published the book *God Alone* with Discovery House.

SCRIPTURE INDEX
OF KEY VERSES

Help us get the word out!

Our Daily Bread Publishing exists to feed the soul with the Word of God.

If you appreciated this book, please let others know.

- Pick up another copy to give as a gift.

- Share a link to the book or mention it on social media.

- Write a review on your blog, on a book-seller's website, or at our own site (odb.org/store).

- Recommend this book for your church, book club, or small group.

Connect with us:

f @ourdailybread

⊙ @ourdailybread

🐦 @ourdailybread

Our Daily Bread Publishing
PO Box 3566
Grand Rapids, Michigan 49501 USA

✉ books@odb.org